Greetings from Ocean Grove, New Jersey

Christopher M. Flynn

Schiffer Publishing Ltd

4880 Lower Valley Road   Atglen, Pennsylvania 19310

7:—Wesley Lake, Ocean Grove, N. J.

Published by Schiffer Publishing Ltd.
4880 Lower Valley Road
Atglen, PA 19310
Phone: (610) 593-1777; Fax: (610) 593-2002
E-mail: Info@schifferbooks.com

For the largest selection of fine reference books on this and related subjects,
please visit our web site at
www.schifferbooks.com
We are always looking for people to write books on new and related subjects. If
you have an idea for a book please contact us at the above address.

This book may be purchased from the publisher.
Include $3.95 for shipping.
Please try your bookstore first.
You may write for a free catalog.

In Europe, Schiffer books are distributed by
Bushwood Books
6 Marksbury Ave.
Kew Gardens
Surrey TW9 4JF England
Phone: 44 (0) 20 8392-8585; Fax: 44 (0) 20 8392-9876
E-mail: info@bushwoodbooks.co.uk
Website: www.bushwoodbooks.co.uk
Free postage in the U.K., Europe; air mail at cost.

Designed by Mark David Bowyer
Type set in BernhardMod BT / Souvenir Lt BT

ISBN: 978-0-7643-2627-1
Printed in China

Contents

Acknowledgments

The existence of this book is due to the help of countless individuals. I would like to thank my aunt, Rosemary English, for providing me with the tools to write the manuscript, and my mom, Cathleen Flynn, for providing me with financial assistance in acquiring postcards and archival materials. Without the aforementioned individuals, this book couldn't have gotten off the ground.

I'd like to thank my wife, Kylene Flynn, and my daughter, Elizabeth Rose, for putting up with my insanity and countless lectures on the history of Ocean Grove.

Last but not least, I'd like to thank those who opened their own collections and archives for me to use: Judy Ryerson, who has an outstanding collection of postcards, and provided me with so many cards for this book that "Thanks to Judy Ryerson!" could have been the sub-title; Rip Mohl, a brilliant organ historian and collector of vintage images, for providing so many of the unique images in this book. And Milton Edelman, one of the surviving photographers from the postcard's golden age, who opened up his incredible repository of original prints and negatives for my use.

Introduction

For a town just a square mile in size, Ocean Grove, New Jersey has an incredible amount of history packed into it. Each average sized thirty-foot by sixty-foot lot has a unique story to tell, since their division by the original Camp Meeting Association Trustees in 1869. What a collection we'd have if only we could get each lot and its buildings to give up all their old ghosts!

It is my challenge as the author to select which groups of ghosts to capture, and how to present them to you, the reader. This book's journey began with the idea that only postcard images would be used to tell the visual portion of the story. That quickly changed.

Postcards were an easy first choice, as they provided a very complete and detailed visual history of so many places in Ocean Grove. Then I was struck with a dilemma; how many times can you show the front of the Auditorium and still keep the readers interested?

That's when I realized that if I began to include photographs, both contemporary and vintage, I could capture a more complete visual story to accompany my text.

So now you, the reader, will get a visual history from many angles, instead of just postcards. When you read about the Sunday parking regulations, a portion of the original blue laws, you'll see a postcard of the gates closed, and a photograph of an original "No Sunday Parking" sign.

I also chose to include a chapter that would provide a brief history and imagery of the immediate neighbors to Ocean Grove. Even though Ocean Grove, surrounded by water on three sides, is nearly an island, it has interacted with the surrounding communities of Asbury Park, Bradley Beach, and Neptune Township. Neptune Township has been an important part of the Ocean Grove story, since the court decision which reversed the Camp Meetings' charter of municipal government in 1979.

I want you, the reader, to understand and appreciate the full story of this fabled and often misunderstood place. At a time when bulldozer beautification is at an alarming rate for such a small, and incredibly historic, location, I hope that you will get a sense of the palpable history that is contained within the borders of Ocean Grove, New Jersey, God's Square Mile of so many different stories.

Chapter One
Greetings From Ocean Grove, New Jersey

In July 1869, a group of Methodist ministers and lay people came upon a parcel of land, bordered on three sides by water, with a high elevation and no mosquitoes. They made a clearing amongst the Cedar trees and scrub pines, pitched their tents, and held their first Camp Meeting. It was July 31st, and born from that meeting was Ocean Grove, New Jersey, God's Square Mile, and the "Queen of the Camp Meetings."

Gathered inside the canvas dwelling of The Reverend Thornley were the people who would create the Ocean Grove Camp Meeting Association. They had been searching up and down the coast line for a suitable place in which to hold their Methodist-based revival meetings and to establish a resort to promote both spiritual and physical well being.

Many of these men, while devout in their faith, also had a keen sense of real estate and business. Soon they began clearing off the wild land, and hiring engineers to begin laying out the street grids, and to survey the lots which this group would soon begin selling leaseholds to.

In December of that year, inside Trinity Methodist Church, Trenton, New Jersey, the group met again, and held the first meeting of the board of trustees. Out of that meeting, they elected the Reverend Ellwood H. Stokes as the Camp Meeting's first president. They established the Board Of Trustees to have thirteen religious and thirteen lay members, and began the task of firmly establishing the community.

In March of 1870, the New Jersey State Legislature granted a municipal charter to the group, in spite of the fact they were a church-based government. (This would finally come to a Supreme Court challenge in 1979.)

The land which Ocean Grove was about to be established on was, at this point, still part of Ocean Township, which is today a distant geographic neighbor. Approximately ten separate tracts of land made up the land between the turnpike, which is now South Main Street/Route 71, and Long Pond and Duck Pond, now Wesley and Fletcher Lakes, respectively. The Association spent $40,000.00 to acquire the parcels of land to create the community.

The Camp Meeting Association soon began selling the leases to their lots, most of which came in the compact size of thirty by sixty feet. Amongst the first people to purchase lots was a business man from New York City by the name of James Bradley, who in a couple of years would be known for establishing Asbury Park, just across Wesley Lake—the northern border of Ocean Grove.

The *Greetings From...*postcard is amongst the simplest of designs for a postcard, yet it has become one of the most enduring and recognizable of them. *Courtesy of Judy Ryerson.*

As part of the organization, the Trustees set forth to write laws, known as blue laws, which would ensure their vision for a proper Christian resort that would promote spiritual and physical well being for the town's residents and visitors. The most famous of these laws was the regulation against the presence of horses and carriages on Sundays, which later expanded its scope to include the horseless carriage, after Henry Ford's invention began to take over the American landscape.

The other blue law which Ocean Grove was known for was the ban against the sale and consumption of alcoholic beverages. This is the only Blue Law that is still partially in effect, as no establishment can sell alcoholic beverages. The law has been lessened to allow the consumption of alcohol in restaurants in the form of *bring your own bottle.*

These blue laws gave Ocean Grove a reputation for being a strict community, firmly rooted in the Methodist faith of the Camp Meeting Association. Despite the occasional snicker or sneer from outsiders, Ocean Grove was, and still is, both a religious and commercial success. Of all the Camp Meetings established during this period of revival, after the country witnessed the horrors of the Civil War, none has survived as intact as Ocean Grove, making it truly, the "Queen of the Camp Meetings."

In these first few years the grounds closed on October 1st, and residents and visitors were not allowed to stay upon the grounds without a permit issued by the chief of police. Caretakers and laborers remained, continuing to clear brush, sand dunes, drill wells, and take care of other chores. Ocean Grove was coming to life.

Large street signs, such as this one from the author's collection, were posted in and around the entrances to Ocean Grove to remind visitors of the *No Sunday Parking* regulations.

This *Greetings From Ocean Grove* postcard, postmarked in 1908, features eight images of various scenes throughout the town. *Courtesy of Judy Ryerson.*

The Railroad Arrives

For the first few years, visitors to Ocean Grove had to travel via train or stagecoach to Long Branch, a few miles to the north. What followed was an often grueling trip by horse and buggy. This all changed in 1875, when the railroad was extended to, and past, Ocean Grove. The flood gates were opened, and soon, literally hundreds of thousands of visitors and potential residents began pouring into the gates of Ocean Grove.

This aerial view of Ocean Grove offers a unique view from the west, looking east, as most are photographed from the opposite direction. Ocean Grove's three natural borders, The Atlantic Ocean, Wesley Lake, and Fletcher Lake, are all shown in this outstanding postcard. *Courtesy Judy Ryerson.*

LAKE PATHWAY.   ASSOCIATION BUILDING.

PIONEER WOMEN VASE.   TENT LIFE.

OCEAN GROVE.

These etchings, taken from a souvenir view book published in 1888, give a sense of the early days in Ocean Grove, before postcards were first published.

One of the most instantly recognizable views of Ocean Grove's history, the Main Avenue gates closed to traffic on Sunday.

The initial scope of the Sunday Blue Laws also included the railroad. No train was allowed to stop within one mile of the community. As a result, a second station was built in northern Asbury Park. This portion of the regulations was short lived, and soon, trains were allowed to stop at the Asbury Park and Ocean Grove railroad station on Sundays.

The railroad brought over 50,000 visitors to the area in the first year, and the station was soon a bustling place of activity, bringing in both people and materials to Ocean Grove, and Asbury Park.

This patriotic themed *Greetings From Ocean Grove* card features a photograph of the boardwalk and beach that helped to draw visitors to the Grove's Camp Meeting in numbers greater than any other during the growth of the Holiness Movement following the Civil War. *Courtesy of Judy Ryerson.*

BOARDWALK
With side view of Coleman House also Plaza Hotel on Lake and Cookman Aves.

A scene on the southern tip of the Asbury Park boardwalk, showing the Auditorium in the distance. Both resorts were proud of their achievements in the use of technology, and this was a relic placed on the boardwalk by James Bradley, to remind visitors of the formerly bumpy carriage ride from Long Branch's train station, which was formerly the *end of the line.*

The original Victorian station was replaced with a more modern brick and concrete station, which opened in November 1922. The elaborate structure, which featured thirty-foot ceilings in the main waiting room, was arguably the most ornate station along the New York and Long Branch Railroad. Sadly, this structure was demolished in March 1978, and was replaced by a rather hideous modern structure, devoid of any architectural detail.

Ocean Grove and Asbury Park Depot, Asbury Park, N. J.

The first railroad station which served Ocean Grove and Asbury Park is shown in this divided back postcard. While the railroad's name was removed from the engine during the coloring process, it is likely from the Pennsylvania Railroad, which served the town along with the Central Railroad of New Jersey.

RAILROAD DEPOT, ASBURY PARK, N. J.

The two smaller structures on either side of the station were used for processing freight and baggage through the station. The children gathered around the crates and other assorted items are likely waiting for the train to arrive, hoping to make some extra spending money by assisting travelers with their luggage. *Courtesy of Judy Ryerson.*

The ornate Ocean Grove and Asbury Park train station shown in this postcard is rumored to have inspired the Lionel toy train company in the design of their model #115 station. *Courtesy of Judy Ryerson.*

193A:—GENERAL VIEW OF R. R. PLAZA AND STATION, ASBURY PARK, N. J.

The linen era *Greetings From…* postcard, as published by the Tichnor Bros., of Boston, Massachusetts. This style of postcard has been an inspiration to countless artists and writers over the years.

Chapter Two
The Ocean Grove
Camp Meeting Association Grounds

Since the goal of the Ocean Grove Camp Meeting Association has always been to promote the Gospel of Christ through the Methodist faith, most of the public buildings that serve secular programs as well as religious are all churches. The oldest of these structures is the Tabernacle, erected and dedicated in 1877.

The Tabernacle, which was dedicated to the memory of Bishop Janes, an early figure in the Ocean Grove Association, began as an octagonal pavilion, with open sides. Eventually, walls were added to the structure, trimmed with Gothic-arched windows. A matching cupola at the top of the building, with double hung windows, provided good ventilation.

Here is the exterior of the Bishop Janes Tabernacle, in an early twentieth century postcard, showing people enjoying the park's natural beauty.

POST OFFICE,
3492   Ocean Grove, N. J.

Located on Main Avenue, the structure which houses Ocean Grove's post office also served as the main offices for the Camp Meeting Association from 1881 through 1971, when they built a new office at the corner of Pitman Avenue and Pilgrim Pathway, overlooking Auditorium Square Park.

An unusual view of the northern side of the Tabernacle is shown in this late 1960s postcard. *Courtesy of Judy Ryerson.*

A later chrome era view of the Youth Temple, one of the last postcards produced of the building before it burned in 1977. *Courtesy of Judy Ryerson.*

Directly across the park from the Tabernacle was, and is again, The Youth Temple. That sentence is worded that way because the original structure, built in 1880, was destroyed by fire in 1977, and a new Victorian-styled multi-purpose structure, also designed for the needs of the youth, was dedicated in 2001.

The original Youth Temple had a capacity of 2,500 people, and was the center of religious activity for Ocean Grove youth for well over a century. The simple open space was also the venue for many memorable Ocean Grove traditions, including the Auditorium Usher's Show. Many shows produced by Ocean Grove youth, as part of the Association's summer programs, also took place in this building.

This view of the eastern façade of the original Youth Temple shows small trees, bare from the winter season. These trees were likely planted as part of an effort to keep the "grove" in Ocean Grove.

14

OCEAN GROVE'S POPULAR
YOUNG PEOPLE'S MEETING
70th ANNIVERSARY YEAR—AUG., 1949—EVERY MORNING AT 9 O'CLOCK
Chorus Choir of Young People — Vocal and Instrumental Soloists

Brief Messages, Vital and Christian

"THIS IS THE PLACE
TO MEET YOUR FRIENDS"

Sow a Thought - Reap an Art
Sow an Act - Reap a Habit
Sow a Habit - Reap a Character
Sow a Character - Reap a Destiny

ROBERT C. WELLS, Leader — WALTER D. EDDOWES, Song Leader
JOSEPHINE EDDOWES, Organist

This postcard, produced to commemorate the seventieth anniversary of the Young People's temple, shows the words of wisdom etched into the minds of the generations who have attended services in this building.

The building was eventually connected to the adjacent cottage which had served as the town's Western Union telegraph office. It was then used for a number of years as classroom space, until the construction of the new Youth Temple.

THORNLEY CHAPEL
Where our Junior Chapel Service for Girls and Boys
is held every morning from 9 to 10 o'clock.
MRS. IDA M. HUDSON, Leader

In this early twentieth century view of Thornley Chapel, a hitching post is visible. *Courtesy of Judy Ryerson.*

While The Youth Temple served older children, the youngest learned their faith in Thornley Chapel. The chapel was built in 1888 as a memorial to the Reverend Joseph Thornley, in whose tent the first prayer service was held in 1869. A simple Victorian chapel, it was expanded in the 1940s to accommodate the increase in youth from the growth of the Baby Boomer generation following World War II.

This unique black and white postcard offers a rare interior view of the addition built onto the western side of the chapel. *Courtesy of Judy Ryerson.*

15

The Great Auditorium

The most important and recognizable of the structures on the Camp Meeting grounds is the Great Auditorium, which replaced a series of two simpler structures. The Auditorium's story begins in 1893, when the Camp Meeting Association announced through New York, Pennsylvania, and New Jersey newspapers a request for plans and construction estimates for an edifice seating 10,000, with the stipulation that it would be ready July 1, 1894.

On September 11, 1893, fifteen architects presented their plans for the new Auditorium, and four finalists were chosen from this group. After much debate, they chose the plans of Fred T. Camp, an architect based in New York City. It was October 10, 1893, and soon after, the plans were finalized, and the "new" Auditorium began to take shape.

Ground was broken for the construction on December 2, 1893, and soon, over 173,943 square feet of material had been excavated to allow the massive foundations of crushed stone, concrete, and granite. By March, 1894, the first iron truss had been lifted into position, and the iron work was completed by the end of the month.

Carpenters followed soon after, adorning the structure with a Victorian flair. A suspended ceiling of Southern Yellow Pine, took shape quickly, enveloping the space, which when completed was 225 feet by 161 feet, making it nearly an acre in size.

This Auditorium was erected in 1880 to replace the small clearing in the brush that had served as the preachers stand. Inadequate for the large numbers of faithful that were coming into Ocean Grove, it was dismantled and replaced with the Great Auditorium.

The Auditorium was one of the first public structures that was illuminated entirely by electric light. Over 1,000 lights were used to illuminate the space, with each one along the arches capable of being pulled through the ceiling, in order to facilitate changing the lamps. Six miles of electrical wire were installed to control the lighting, leading to electrical regulators located in fire-proof vaults in the Auditorium's basement.

Looking eastward from the rear of the Auditorium, shown here are the massive steel beams which support the vast open space of the structure.

A view of the front of the Auditorium under construction, following the completion of the steel work in March 1894. In this image, the shortest of the three towers on the eastern façade of the structure are starting to take shape.

The primary reason Ellwood Stokes commissioned the Auditorium's construction was that crowds had outgrown the capacity of the preacher's stand. The idea of a larger auditorium had been considered for five years prior, according to remarks made by Dr. Stokes in Camp Meeting reports of the time. The new structure meant, and continues to mean, that Ocean Grove could attract the best in both religious and secular programming.

With elaborate decorations in place, this postcard depicts a children's pageant before the choir loft was remodeled to accommodate the Hope-Jones organ in 1908. *Courtesy of Judy Ryerson.*

The exterior of the Auditorium, shortly after completion in July, 1894. The front of the building would later be changed and enlarged in 1908, when the Hope-Jones organ was installed in the building.

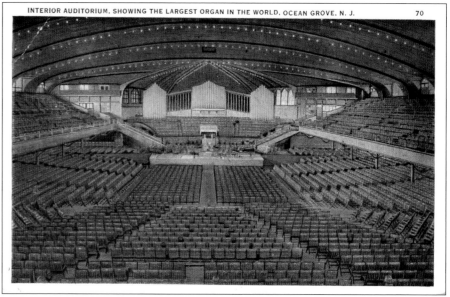

The interior of the Auditorium, shown in a white-border postcard, circa 1920. The fan-like pattern of the seats in the Auditorium was meant to show that the word of God being preached from the pulpit would carry with the congregation out into the world.

A Legacy of Preachers and Performers

Of all the Camp Meetings that sprung up during the post Civil War period, none ever quite gained the notoriety of Ocean Grove, nor has any endured over the years like Ocean Grove. These two factors, combined with the excellent facilities available to both secular and religious program presenters, has allowed Ocean Grove's Auditorium to attract a diverse legacy of ministers, performers, and musicians.

The Auditorium exterior by night, with the outline of the structure, and the adjacent pavilion, outlined in miniature white lights. This method of illumination, while not consistent with the Victorian architecture, was made popular by the amusement park architecture of places like Luna Park, Coney Island.

42375

Greetings from Ocean Grove, N. J.

This chrome postcard from the late 1960s shows the Memorial Cross on the front of the building. Visible for over a mile out to sea, it is illuminated each night, and is featured in a lighting ceremony each June, which signifies the opening of the Camp Meeting Association for the summer.

19

OCEAN GROVE, N. J.

THE AUDITORIUM

The doors are swung wide
  open,

The choir is in its place,

The Ministers on the platform

Are praying now for Grace.

The people filling the spaces

Listen with pious mien,

Singing their hallelujahs

To God the Father, unseen.

(c) *Effie M. Anderson.*

Poetry cards like this are unique variations on a standard postcard.
This white border view is circa 1925.

"Ladies and Gentlemen, Presenting …"
Entertainment in Ocean Grove

For over 110 years, the top names in Entertainment have been drawn to the stage of the Great Auditorium, owing a great deal to the unique atmosphere and wonderful acoustics of the structure. The building's stage has seen almost every form of popular music since Reverend Stokes dedicated the building in 1894, even branching out into rock-n-roll, despite a rocky start in that genre in the 1960s.

The earliest performers in the Auditorium included a who's who of late nineteenth and early twentieth century opera stars. The famed Enrico Caruso became a traditional seasonal favorite in the Auditorium, with his tenor voice echoing off the curved pine ceiling. Caruso's popularity as an Opera singer in Ocean Grove was split with Galla Curci, who also conquered a crowd of 10,000 without any amplification.

REV. WM. A. SUNDAY, EVANGELIST.

The Reverend Billy Sunday is depicted in this white border postcard. *Courtesy of Judy Ryerson.*

The Reverend Norman Vincent Peale is depicted in this real photograph postcard. An Ocean Grove tradition over the years, he preached his last public sermon in the building in 1991.

The staunch Methodist heritage of nearly 100 years that existed when rock 'n' roll took over the American landscape in the 1950s and 1960s, delayed the appearance of it in the Auditorium until the 1970s. Since that time period, the Auditorium has hosted a who's who of late twentieth century popular entertainment, including: Bob Hope, Tony Bennett, The Lettermen, Seals and Croft, Bill Cosby, The Preservation Hall Jazz Band, Tony Orlando, Mel Torme, Peter, Paul, and Mary, Garrison Keilor, Victor Borge, The Stars of the Lawrence Welk Television Show, and countless Doo-Wop groups from the 1950s and 1960s.

John McCormack, celebrated Irish tenor, and party on Great Northern Oriental Limited Diner.

From 1921 this post-card depicts Caruso, surrounded by a border, which pays tribute to his Italian-American heritage. *Courtesy of Judy Ryerson.*

ENRICO CARUSO
ITALIAN AMERICAN
FIRST TENOR

POST CARD

GREAT
NORTHERN
RAILWAY
Glacier National Park

"See America First"

and Don't Fail to Hear
John McCormack
at the Ocean Grove Auditorium
Saturday Night
August 7, 1915
Prices: $2.00, $1.50, $1.00 and 75c.
Now on sale.
Fifty cent seats on sale night of concert.

See Glacier National Park
The grandeur of the scenes seen there
You'll carry with you—everywhere.

This post card was produced to advertise an appearance by John McCormack, an early recording star. The verso of the card, also shown here, shows the ticket prices, common for events of this time period. The fifty-cent seats on sale the night of the event were likely the far rear balcony.

In addition to secular music, in recent years, contemporary Christian music has become a popular draw for the Auditorium. Produced in conjunction with major New York area Christian radio stations, these events have drawn many of the top names in this genre of music, including: The Newsboys, Audio Adrenaline, Jars of Clay, and Grammy award winner Michael W. Smith.

Peter, Paul and Mary

Peter, Paul, and Mary, folk music legends, have become an Ocean Grove tradition in recent years, like Sousa and Caruso two generations ago. The group's rendition of the folk standard, *We Shall Overcome,* is often accompanied by the Auditorium's massive pipe organ, bringing the entire crowd to their feet.

This unique card depicts John Phillip Sousa, with the elaborate border on the card depicting various musical and artistic symbols, including the five muses, shown at the card's top. *Courtesy of Judy Ryerson.*

One of the many annual events held in the Auditorium is the Neptune Township High School graduation. Graduates are always thrilled to end their high school careers to the strains of Pomp and Circumstance played on the Hope-Jones organ. Additional music is traditionally provided by the school's band, which plays in the area between the stage and the altar rail.

Ocean Grove has also been the sight of many visits by important political figures, as well as social events, including, speeches by several United States presidents, including Roosevelt, McKinley, and Nixon. Nearly every New Jersey Governor has spoken from the stage, including Governor Stokes, who was a distant relative of the Association's first President.

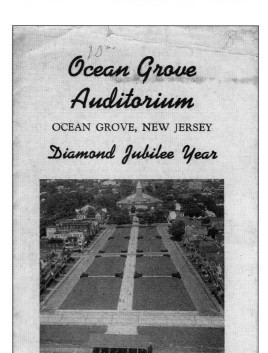

A program announcing events for Ocean Grove's Diamond Jubilee season in 1944, which included reminders to pray for the soldiers overseas and to maintain the Sunday parking regulations.

The giant American flag in front of the organ pipes is festooned with hundreds of clear light bulbs, which, when lit, give the illusion that it is waving in a breeze. *Courtesy of Christopher Fodge.*

A vintage Sunday bulletin from the Auditorium.

The Legendary Hope-Jones Pipe Organ

The story of the Auditorium's organ begins in 1895, when a mechanical action organ was donated to the Camp Meeting Association from Washington Square Methodist Episcopal Church, New York City. The organ and its enclosed case were used for just under ten years, when it became clear that this instrument was inadequate for a number of reasons. The decision was made to move this organ into The Youth Temple and to contract with an organ builder for a new instrument for the Auditorium.

Tali Esen Morgan, who was the musical director in Ocean Grove, contracted with Robert Hope-Jones, an English organ builder who had recently come to America. This simple business agreement in 1907, set forth a dynasty which lead to the Ocean Grove Auditorium having one of the world's most renowned pipe organs.

The last President who visited the Ocean Grove Auditorium was Richard M. Nixon in 1973. The crowds amassed in this photograph would soon witness the Air-Force One helicopter landing on Ocean Pathway, followed by Nixon addressing a capacity crowd in the historic edifice.

President Roosevelt always addressed a full Auditorium, shown here in this card postmarked in 1908. *Courtesy of Judy Ryerson.*

417- PRESIDENT ROOSEVELT DELIVERING ADDRESS AUDITORIUM, OCEAN GROVE.

Hope-Jones is regarded as one of the greatest innovators in the world of pipe organs over the last 100 years. He was responsible for perfecting the use of electricity to control pipe organs, and invented a number of different pipes, such as the Diaphone, which is an extremely large bass producing pipe.

The Hope-Jones organ façade shortly after the instruments installation in 1908.

This chrome era view shows the Auditorium filled to capacity, which was 9,000 before the original seating on the main floor was updated with padded theater-style seats in 1961. This change brought the building to its current capacity, 6,500. *Courtesy of Judy Ryerson.*

In 1930, the organ was in need of repairs, and this work was undertaken by Earl J. Beach, who studied organ building with Hope-Jones, and was involved in the original installation in 1908. Beach replaced the leather inside the organ chests, replaced the console, and began an expansion program that continues indefinitely!

This expansion was followed shortly by the installation of a set of chimes in 1940. This set of chimes was installed in a glass case alongside the main floor of the Auditorium. The chime's playing was amplified and could be broadcast from the main tower at the center of the Auditorium. The Camp Meeting Association was very proud of the chimes, and the advanced technology used in their production and installation, evident by the number of promotional flyers that mention them.

It was at the beginning of this time period that Ocean Grove also contracted with a new organist to undertake the playing of the massive instrument. In 1925, Clarence Kholmann, who was born and trained in Philadelphia, Pennsylvania, took over from the first Ocean Grove organist, Clarence Reynolds. Kholmann carried on the tradition of playing, *The Storm*, a descriptive piece that used many of the unique sound effects installed in the organ. This piece, arranged by Reynolds, included the effects of wind, rain, thunder, and lighting, set to the tune of many patriotic and religious songs played on the organ.

Kholmann also left a lasting mark on the Auditorium and its corps of volunteer ushers. He penned the Ocean Grove Auditorium Ushers March, which the ushers have used ever since to march to the altar rail, carrying the offering from the congregation during the services.

The installation of new organ pipes often requires a great deal of man power and machinery, such as this scene which unfolded during the installation of the 32' Contra-Tibia.

Clarence Kholmann served as the Auditorium organist through 1944, when he passed away in December of that year. Josephine Eddows, whose husband was already serving as musical director, was appointed as his replacement in March 1945.

During this time period, the organ continued to expand. An echo organ was installed in a chamber above the Auditorium ceiling, as a memorial to Clarence Kholmann. The Beach Organ Company installed a second console, and it continued to serve the congregation well, until the 1970s.

Due to various mitigating circumstances, a number of problems cropped up during this time period. One of the greatest losses during this time was the original diaphone. Being the prototype for this rank of pipes caused a great number of problems, and the pipes literally beat themselves to death. The great rank had gone silent.

So in a set of fortunate circumstances, entered a man who many consider to be the savior of the Ocean Grove organ, John R. Shaw. He had been crawling around in the organ since he was a little boy, when Beech would take him around the instrument, showing him the mysterious inner workings of the instrument. Mr. Shaw took over as curator of the instrument, and set forth an expansion and restoration program. Solving the problems of the now silent diaphones became a major priority for the Auditorium organ.

Hope-Jones had installed a diaphone of similar scale and wind pressure in Philadelphia's Baptist Temple, which was at this time closed and slated for demolition. Shaw managed to secure the diaphone and other pipes from the building, and moved the entire set of pipes to Ocean Grove for restoration and reinstallation. This was no small task, as the largest pipe was thirty-two feet long and weighed one ton.

For nearly thirty years now, Dr. Gordon Turk has been the master of this magnificent instrument. A graduate of the Curtis Institute of Music, he has recorded several albums on the organ and is featured in weekly recitals during July and August. In the winter months, his concert schedule has included tours of Russia and Japan, in addition to his duties as organist to St. Mary's Episcopal Church, Wayne, PA.

The Auditorium Ushers have brought the collection to the platform for years to the accompaniment of this piece of sheet music, the *Auditorium Ushers' March*. This unique presentation features actual ushers during the 1940s as part of the musical notation. *Courtesy of Rip Mohl.*

Perhaps the most famous organist of all time, Virgil Fox, played a number of recitals over the years in Ocean Grove. He is shown here in one of his last full public recitals in Ocean Grove before passing away from cancer. *Courtesy of John Shaw.*

The Tenting Way of Life

Ocean Grove vacation lodgings range from ornate Victorian palaces to simple canvas tents with cottages attached at the rear.

The Auditorium ushers are depicted taking up the Sunday offering in this linen era card which was postmarked in 1946.

A view of the tent community beside the northwest corner of the Auditorium, at the foot of one of the many Biblical-named streets in Ocean Grove, Mt. Pisgah Way. *Courtesy of Judy Ryerson.*

The tent community is the oldest form of vacation housing in Ocean Grove, dating back to the very first meetings held in July 1869. At the peak of tenting in Ocean Grove, nearly 400 canvas tents with wooden rear cottages could be found around Ocean Grove. The first large section of the tenting grounds to be converted into something other than tents was at the North End Hotel, which in 1911 replaced that portion of the tent community, known as Bethesda Block.

A rare private mailing card showing the tents, surrounded in a lush grove of trees. This card was sent to a resident of Pitman Grove, New Jersey, another Camp Meeting in the state, and is postmarked in July 1898, making it one of the earliest Ocean Grove postcards in existence.

29

A further portion of the tent community was replaced in 1945 when the Association donated land for the construction of Francis Asbury Manor along the shores of Fletcher Lake. Still other locations were converted into private cottages, with a traditional framed building replacing the canvas.

The 114 remaining tents are now centered around the Auditorium and Camp Meeting Grounds. Despite the occasional high-speed Internet access connection, and indoor plumbing, very little has changed about tenting for over 130 years. The traditional occupation date of May 15th through September 15th has remained, as too has the design of the exterior of the tent, with scalloped edging along the front wall, set off by a colorful canopy for the porch roof.

Each of the tents is removed for the winter months, and stored in the rear cabin, along with the occupant's furniture and other miscellaneous personal belongings. When the time comes to erect them again, beginning in mid-April, the tents are unrolled and they are hoisted by a dedicated group of Camp Meeting Association maintenance personnel. The original tent poles were created from Cedar logs felled right in Ocean Grove, and several older Cedar poles still remain in use today. When repairs dictate replacement, this is one of the only areas where a modern building material, pressure- treated lumber, is used to insure historical acuracy.

A recent fire destroyed three tent cabins in the off season. In order to meet building codes, since this was the first time an entire cabin had to be replaced in a very long time, they were designed and built like condominiums. Jack Green Homes, Kearny, New Jersey, undertook this unique project. Featuring the only level floors in the tent community, the addition of fire walls does little to affect the appearance of the tents, as they blend in seamlessly with the older tents and their cottages.

For those desiring less rustic summer lodging, the Association also maintains a stable of cottages, which are leased by families from generation to generation, just as in the tent community. While these were once spread throughout Ocean Grove, only two blocks remain, the remainder having been converted into private homes. In the current grouping, located on Surf and Bath Avenues, their bead-board siding with fresh white paint and green trim makes them instantly recognizable as the Camp Meting's cottages.

Not all the cottages in this group began as such; on the Bath Avenue side of the community is a two-story brick building. This structure was erected in 1881, using surplus materials from the construction of the Association Building on Main Avenue. The structure's original purpose was to store tools and materials used by the Association's building and grounds crew. Very little has changed in the interior of the structure, now rented as a two-family home as part of the tent and cottage community. Even the original fuse boxes, made of wood and lined with lead, are still in the walls, as are several earlier gas lines.

Postmarked in 1909, this lithographed card depicts the North End tent community shortly before it was removed to make way for the North End Hotel complex. *Courtesy of Judy Ryerson.*

This hand-colored view of the North End tent community is postmarked in 1907, and is mislabeled as an Asbury Park view, a common occurrence for cards depicting scenes in and around Wesley Lake. *Courtesy of Judy Ryerson.*

3:—Tents and Auditorium, Ocean Grove, N. J.

These tents are located along Mt. Zion Way, which is located directly behind the southwestern corner of the Auditorium.

This real photo postcard depicts the tents along Pilgrim Pathway, which are known as Bethany Block.

AVENUE OF TENTS
3494   Ocean Grove, N. J.

Campus, Ocean Grove, N. J.

A unique view of the tents in the early spring, prior to the Association's building and grounds crew setting the giant canvas into place.

AVENUE OF TENTS, OCEAN GROVE, N. J.

Arthur Livingston, Publisher, New York.   238

Tent Life, Ocean Grove, N. J.

An Arthur Livingston card showing the tents alongside the Auditorium, which are known as Front Circle. Due to their proximity to the Auditorium, these are among the most sought after tents in the entire tent community.

Shown in this view are a wicker baby stroller, and a few bicycles, evidence of children enjoying a happy summer in Ocean Grove. *Courtesy of Judy Ryerson.*

Hand-colored postcards from Arthur Livingston are comparatively rare, as most of his cards were based on untouched black and white photography. These cards capture the brightness of the actual colors used in both history and in the present day. *Courtesy of Judy Ryerson.*

AVENUE OF TENTS, OCEAN GROVE, N.J.

ARTHUR LIVINGSTON, N. Y. No. 650.

My dear Eugenie, I came here after all. — Flora

Tent Dwelling, Ocean Grove, N.J.

24055

The corner tent facing the Jerusalem Pavilion is one of the most photographed tents over the generations in Ocean Grove. This hand-colored card depicts a dazzling array of flowers planted by this tent's occupants. *Courtesy of Judy Ryerson.*

Behind The Scenes

The success of the Ocean Grove Camp Meeting Association is directly correlated to the many faithful men and women who have served it for over 130 years. As with many religious organizations, the people offering their dedicated service are a mixture of paid employees and volunteers.

The heart of the Association has been the board of trustees, which started as the core group of people who first met on the grounds in July 1869. When they elected the first group of trustees they chose Elwood H. Stokes as the first president of the Camp Meeting Association. He was born in Medford, New Jersey, and worked in the book binding trade until he entered the ministry of the Methodist church at the age of twenty-five. Stokes was an accomplished author and poet, authoring two volumes of poetry inspired by Ocean Grove, and a third inspired by his trip to Europe.

Stokes' vision for Ocean Grove was largely responsible for many of the traditions and buildings still in place 137 years later. It was under his leadership that saw the construction of the town's greatest religious and architectural achievement, The Auditorium. It has often been said that Ocean Grove was truly this man's greatest achievement.

When he passed away in his home in Ocean Grove, on July 16, 1897, his body was transported to the Auditorium, were he lay in state for three days, until his funeral services were held on July 19th in the building he was known for. To date, this is the only funeral service that has been held in building.

While some smaller volunteer groups may have come and gone, two core groups of volunteers, The Auditorium Ushers and the Ladies Auxiliary of Auditorium Ushers, have been tremendous assets to Ocean Grove for well over 100 years.

122:—Tent City, Ocean Grove, N. J.

Strange looking trees are prominent in this white border era view depicting the tents along Fletcher Lake, the southern end of Ocean Grove. *Courtesy of Judy Ryerson.*

Rev. Ellwood H. Stokes, D. D., LL. D.

BORN, OCTOBER 10th, 1815,
DIED, JULY 16th, 1897.

———:———

Funeral Services Held in the Auditorium,

OCEAN GROVE, N. J.,

Monday, July 19th, 1897, 2 P. M.

BISHOP JAMES N. FITZGERALD, D. D., LL. D., Presiding.

The program for Stokes' funeral, a rare, albeit morbid Ocean Grove collectible.

A Well Called Beersheba

Many of the early Camp Meeting Association reports and advertisements mention the number of deep artesian wells drilled on the grounds of the Association. None of these wells received the notoriety that Ocean Grove's first well has—Beersheba, located in Auditorium Square Park. A small Victorian gazebo was erected at the sight and a cast-iron drinking fountain was installed, looking ornate enough to be an ornamental fountain rather than a drinking fountain. The well's name is yet another site in Ocean Grove which takes influence from Biblical text, this time, the Book of Genesis.

Drinking at the Beersheba Well, Ocean Grove, N. J.   221

BEERSHEBA
First Well Driven in Ocean Grove
JUNE 1870

PHOTO BY AGREEN   88240

Beersheba Well is depicted in this "linen" postcard, circa 1940.

An earlier view of the well, which also serves as the logo for the Historical Society of Ocean Grove.

The Well, Ocean Grove, N. J.

Chapter Three
Home Away From Home

Now that wireless Internet access is offered by many hotels as a guest amenity, it is hard to imagine that a leading advertising feature often drawn upon by hoteliers of the past was the presence of hot- and cold-running water. Private baths are still a comparative rarity in Ocean Grove's hotels when compared to other resorts. This unique blend creates the hotel, inn, motel, and bed and breakfast landscape of Ocean Grove.

The Ocean Plaza was lovingly restored in 1994 by its current owners, Jack and Valerie Green. The restoration's craftsmanship was at such a high level, many people in town now refer to it as a touchstone for perfect restoration standards.

MAIN AVENUE HOUSE 19 Main Ave., Ocean Grove, N. J. Phone Asbury Park 7229. H. E. Clark, Propr.

The Main Avenue House, known now as the Majestic, recently under went a complete restoration. It houses a fine restaurant and hotel within its ornate Victorian walls.

HOME-LIKE LOBBY   OVERLOOKING THE SEA

Announcing the Opening on May 26th for 1949

Shawmont, Ocean Grove, N. J.

RESERVATIONS ACCEPTED IN ADVANCE

I. A. Shaw, Owner   Tel. Asbury Park 2-4984   E. S. Norris, Mgr.

Interior views, such as this one showing the ornate Victorian lobby of the Shawmont Hotel, are harder to find than exterior views. This is likely due to the cumbersome nature of early flash photography equipment.

HOTEL BATH AVENUE HOUSE, 37 Bath Ave., Cor. Central, OCEAN GROVE, NEW JERSEY

An unusual blue tint was applied to this postcard of the Bath Avenue House, located at the corner of Central and Bath Avenues, near Founders' Park. This hotel is significant for the author, as it was one of the first places his family stayed when they first "discovered" Ocean Grove in the early 1960s.

The Spray View Hotel, now converted into condos, is shown in this early 1950s chrome postcard.

The Bellaire, located on Ocean Pathway, is an example of a structure now used as a single family home, with a heritage as a hotel or rooming house.

BELLAIRE, 24 Ocean Pathway, Ocean Grove, N. J.

The Ocean Grove Motor Inn has been converted into rental apartments and professional office space. It was also the one and only motel to ever be built in Ocean Grove.

39

The Cordova Hotel, located on Webb Avenue, has been restored in recent years. Neon signs, like the one over the hotel's entrance, have since been prohibited under zoning statute, as they are not consistent with the town's historic atmosphere.

The Hotel Whitfield, Surf Avenue, is now used as an apartment building, and maintains much of the original detail today as is shown on this postcard from the mid-1950s.

The Park View Hotel, located on Seaview Avenue, is another hotel that has been lovingly restored and preserved over the years. It is also one of the largest hotels still operating as a hotel, as the structure continues through to Wesley Lake and Lake Avenue, which runs parallel to the lake.

Seaside Hotel, Ocean Grove, N. J.

The Seaside Hotel, Ocean Avenue, was converted into condominiums in the late 1980s. A lone automobile stands waiting at the curb in this early twentieth century hand-colored view.

SURF AVENUE HOUSE — 27 SURF AVE. — OCEAN GROVE, NEW JERSEY

The Surf Avenue House, aptly located on Surf Avenue, was saved by fire fighters when the adjacent Fountain House hotel burnt in 1918.

The Fountain House, located on Central Avenue, had a capacity of 350 guests.

This card was produced for the name change of the Sheldon House to the Fountain House. *Courtesy of Judy Ryerson.*

THE FOUNTAIN HOUSE, (Formerly The Sheldon) OCEAN GROVE, N. J.

Facing park, one block from ocean. New management; newly furnished; near Auditorium and Casino. Private baths. Capacity 350; table unexcelled; special rates to families. Booklet furnished.

FOUNTAIN HOTEL CO.

Where Grandma boarded at the Friends Conference in July 1910.

BOARDWALK AND NORTH END HOTEL.   OCEAN GROVE, N. J.

The North End Hotel, demolished in the late 1970s, is shown in this rare sepia-toned postcard. A developer has recently signed an agreement with the Camp Meeting Association to rebuild a hotel and condominium development at the sight which will pay homage to the original structure. *Courtesy of Judy Ryerson.*

Hotel Arlington, Ocean Grove, N. J.

The ornate Arlington Hotel occupied an entire square block of real estate between Pilgrim Pathway and Central Avenue. It was demolished in the late 1960s to make way for one of the first condominium complexes in New Jersey.

The eastern half of the Arlington's main lobby, which in this rare postcard, shows off the hotel's plush Victorian-era furnishings.*Courtesy of Judy Ryerson.*

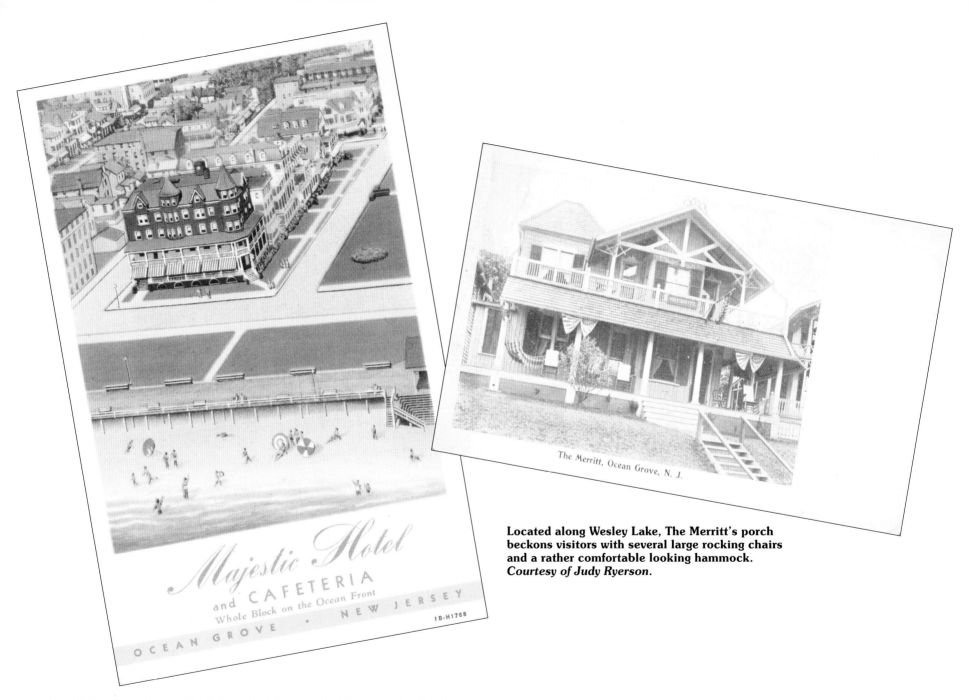

The Merritt, Ocean Grove, N. J.

Located along Wesley Lake, The Merritt's porch beckons visitors with several large rocking chairs and a rather comfortable looking hammock. *Courtesy of Judy Ryerson.*

Majestic Hotel and CAFETERIA
Whole Block on the Ocean Front
OCEAN GROVE • NEW JERSEY

1B-H1788

The Majestic, and several adjoining hotels, were lost in a massive fire in the 1970s. Victorian single-family homes occupy the site today, built to blend with existing architecture.

Many of the structures that either previously or currently serve the town as hotels are among the most ornate in terms of architecture and size. Some of the architecturally significant hotels, such as the Ardmore and Summerfield Hotels (Ocean Pathway), have been lost to fire. Many of the significant ones that have been restored are the Ocean Plaza (Ocean Pathway), The Aurora (Surf Avenue), The Manchester (Ocean Pathway), and The Cordova (Webb Avenue).

BREAKERS
SURF AVENUE AT THE OCEAN
OCEAN GROVE, N. J.

The Breakers spent a number of years as a rooming house with deinstitutionalized mental patients as the primary occupants. It was demolished by the State of New Jersey after the patient's were relocated, as part of an effort to lessen the burden on towns with an over abundance of this form of housing. *Courtesy of Judy Ryerson.*

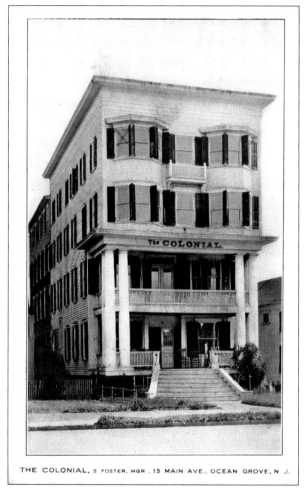

THE COLONIAL, S FOSTER, MGR, 15 MAIN AVE., OCEAN GROVE, N J.

Mr. and Mrs. Wm. J. Brunning, 18 Seaview Ave., Ocean Grove, N. J. 07756

The Cornwall House   Telephone (201) 775-1513

The Colonial was located on Main Avenue, and was partially destroyed by fire in the 1980s. It was rebuilt following the fire and converted into condominiums, with the structure still maintaining the massive columns on the front porch. *Courtesy of Judy Ryerson.*

The Cornwall House has since been converted into a private residence and is lovingly cared for by its present owners. *Courtesy of Judy Ryerson.*

The Boscobel Hotel has been restored, and is currently used as an apartment building. Retail space is located in the basement and the former first floor lobby spaces, as shown here on this unique card. *Courtesy of Judy Ryerson.*

The massive Alaska hotel was located at 3 through 5 Pitman Avenue. The simple iron railings surrounding the property from which the photograph was taken are characteristic of Ocean Grove fences in the late nineteenth and early twentieth centuries. *Courtesy of Judy Ryerson.*

The Dun-Haven Hotel, located on Ocean Pathway, was destroyed in the great fire which took many neighboring hotels with it. The verso of this chrome era postcard advertises the building having elevator service, a rarity in Ocean Grove's Victorian hotel stock. *Courtesy of Judy Ryerson.*

Furnished Rooms

92 MT. ZION WAY

OCEAN GROVE, N. J.

—

Have been spending three very pleasant weeks here. I did not fail to take my daily dip in the big ocean. Its great. Now I'm getting ready to leave for the Mts!

HA Crowell

This card depicts 92 Mt. Zion Way, a prime example of a private home used as a rooming house in order to catch some of the lucrative business available during the summer season. This card's unique feature is that it is printed on pre-stamped stock, purchased from the United States Post Office. *Courtesy of Judy Ryerson.*

The sender of this card, postmarked in 1922, remarks that the Grand Atlantic Hotel serves meals to 2,500 people a day, a prime example of the popularity of Ocean Grove during this time period. *Courtesy of Judy Ryerson.*

The Grand Atlantic Hotel

OCEAN GROVE, N. J.

M. J. WOODRING, OWNER

PHONE, ASBURY PARK 1476

EUROPEAN PLAN

CAFETERIA SERVICE

CAPACITY 250

EL DORADO, Ocean Grove, N. J.   D. W. FISHER,

The El Dorado, located on Broadway, was lost to fire in the 1950s, and was replaced with two single-family homes. *Courtesy of Judy Ryerson.*

The Elim Cottage, located on Main Avenue, was run as a low-cost boarding home for visiting members of other Christian denomination clergy who wished to visit Ocean Grove. It was managed by a dedicated group of women who also ran fundraisers to help offset the costs incurred in the operation of the facility. *Courtesy of Judy Ryerson.*

In studying early postcards, one also notices that a number of structures thought of today as private homes, began life as hotels and rooming houses. It is common to find individual sinks in many bedrooms, an indicator of their vacation lodging heritage. These early postcards can also be an important visual reference towards restoring original Victorian architectural elements that have been lost to the ages.

The study of these postcards also shows how important the historical preservation regulations in Ocean Grove are. The Ocean Grove Motor Inn, while a prime example of 1950s motel-style architecture, is not harmonious with the town's Victorian heritage. In recent years, the structure, now converted to apartments, has been modified with landscaping and decorative elements to blend better with the surroundings.

Postcards have also served as indicators of social trends in vacationing, as in the last forty years, people have shifted towards day trips along with the improvements in highway access. A great deal of this shift is due to the opening of the Garden State Parkway, which affected a great number of New Jersey seashore resorts in a variety of negative, and positive, ways.

This factor also brings up a subject of great difficulty for Ocean Grove in the recent past. Many of these hotels, no longer filled by vacationers, were converted into residential healthcare facilities for mentally ill individuals. This was all due to a variety of complex social and political issues, not appropriate for this text. These conversions led to an over saturation of deinstitutionalized residents being placed in Ocean Grove. New regulations were introduced by the State of New Jersey in the 1990s which better regulated this type of housing. This greatly helped Ocean Grove's image and residents. Today, only a handful of these hotel and boarding house conversions remain, and the residents in them live in harmony with the rest of Ocean Grove, a testament to the tolerance shown in this Christian resort.

The Ardmore Summerfield Hotel, one of the architectural gems in Ocean Grove lost to fire in the 1970s.

Group portraits were often captured on the wide porches that Ocean Grove is known for. *Courtesy of Judy Ryerson.*

A cast-iron finial adorns the roof top of the Lane Villa Hotel shown in this postcard. *Courtesy of Judy Ryerson.*

A drainage pipe runs down the side of this hotel, a practice often seen throughout Ocean Grove and other communities in the early twentieth century; as plumbing technology advanced, often there was no other place to run the pipes. *Courtesy of Judy Ryerson.*

The Lillagaard Hotel, Abbott Avenue, is one of the most recognizable hotel facades preserved in Ocean Grove today. The three towers across the front of the building are instantly recognizable from aerial views. *Courtesy of Judy Ryerson.*

This card produced by the La Pierre Hotel advertises the room rates on the verso of the card, which ranged from $6.00 to $12.50 a night, depending on whether a room had running water, a half bath, or a full bath. *Courtesy of Judy Ryerson.*

FRONT ENTRANCE—4 SEAVIEW AVE.   OCEAN GROVE, N. J.   REAR ENTRANCE—3 ATLANTIC AVE.

The St. George featured a unique pair of turrets as the rear entrance to the hotel. *Courtesy of Judy Ryerson.*

SHORE-VIEW HOTEL, OCEAN PATHWAY AT BEACH AVE., OCEAN GROVE, N. J.
PHONE ASBURY PARK 8436
C. B. ROHLAND, OWNERSHIP-MANAGEMENT

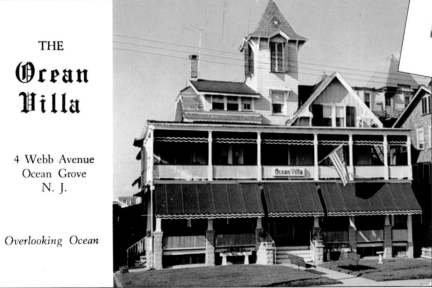

THE

Ocean
Villa

4 Webb Avenue
Ocean Grove
N. J.

Overlooking Ocean

The Shore View, is shown in this sepia-toned postcard. The simple three-story structure to the rear of the hotel appears to be an early twentieth century addition. *Courtesy of Judy Ryerson.*

The Ocean Villa was demolished in the 1980s, after its distinctive cupola was removed for restoration and placement in Auditorium Square Park, where it serves as a tourism information center. *Courtesy of Judy Ryerson.*

SUNSET LODGE   Central and Pitman Avenues   Ocean Grove, N. J.
                200 YARDS FROM OCEAN

The Sunset Lodge, is
shown in this divided
back era postcard.

Unusual triangular windows adorn the
dormers on the Virginia hotel, shown in
this real photo postcard. The neighboring
houses are all Craftsmen-style homes built
in the 1920s, a common replacement for
housing and hotel stock, which burned
in the early part of the twentieth century.
Courtesy Judy Ryerson.

THE VIRGINIA, OCEAN GROVE, NEW JERSEY

VIRGINIA

RICE VILLA, Ocean Grove, N. J.

The Rice Villa's intricate fretwork and birdlike swooping roofline are elements often seen in Victorian architecture. Also of note are the hand-painted street signs on the telephone pole on the left side of the image. *Courtesy of Judy Ryerson.*

The Pathway Manor, lost to fire in the 1970s, had a stamp with their hotel's name applied to assist in finding it in a sea of delicate and wonderful Victorian architecture. *Courtesy of Judy Ryerson.*

Pittsburg House, Ocean Grove, N. J.

OCEAN VIEW HOTEL

CORNER BROADWAY & CENTRAL AVENUE
OCEAN GROVE, N. J.
"The Coolest Spot in Ocean Grove"

Private
Baths
Showers

European
Plan

Television
Lounge

Near
Restaurants

Twenty-Fifth Season 1959 - May 22 to September 14

The Ocean View Hotel was formerly located on the corner of Broadway and Central Avenue. *Courtesy of Judy Ryerson.*

The sender of this card, postmarked in 1911, was staying the summer at this hotel, the Pittsburg House.

The Roosevelt, cor. Beach and Atlantic Ave's., one block from the Ocean. Open from June 1st. Convenient to First-Class Hotels.—Miss L. A. Hoferkamp, Ocean Grove, N. J.

The Roosevelt, with striped awnings and delicate ginger bread trim, is shown in this early hand-colored postcard. *Courtesy of Judy Ryerson.*

The Marine Hotel's exterior featured wide porches and a slate-covered Mansard roof. The building has since been converted into apartments and professional office space. *Courtesy of Judy Ryerson.*

With its wide lawns, the Windamar has been a popular retreat for Ocean Grove visitors for generations. *Courtesy of Judy Ryerson.*

"HOUSE OF COMFORT"

THE NATIONAL

56 MAIN AVENUE, OCEAN GROVE, N. J.

AMERICAN AND EUROPEAN

RESIDENT MANAGER
MARY F. O'NEILL

ASSOCIATE MANAGER
EASTON Z. BEARE

The National was located on Main Avenue, as shown in this divided back postcard postmarked in 1922. *Courtesy of Judy Ryerson.*

Norman House
28-34 Bath Ave.,
OCEAN GROVE,
N. J.

The Norman House, which occupied a number of 30 x 60 foot lots, is a prime example of two buildings being joined together to form one hotel structure. This was often a practice in Ocean Grove. *Courtesy of Judy Ryerson.*

THE WILMINGTON, HENRY BECKER, PROP. 44 HECK AVENUE, OCEAN GROVE, N. J.

Hotel postcards often included a large gathering of guests posing to have their photograph taken, as shown in this real photo postcard of the Wilmington Hotel. *Courtesy of Judy Ryerson.*

Greetings from **THE OCEANIC HOTEL**

34 Beach Avenue

Cor. Pitman Avenue

(OCEAN BLOCK)

All Outside Rooms

Hot and Cold
Running Water

European Plan

Reasonable Rates

Tel. PRospect 5-9755

SYDNEY A. TERHUNE
Owner

THE OCEANIC HOTEL, OCEAN GROVE, N. J.

Hotels often modernized their exteriors in the early and mid-twentieth century, prior to historic zoning regulations, such as the Oceanic Hotel, which put stucco on the formerly Victorian exterior.

Various hotel advertisements always specify whether the hotel offered American or European dining plans, and some offered both. The American Plan included all meals, and the European plan meant that all meals were at an extra cost. Visitors who took the latter plan had plentiful choices in the many fine restaurants in both historic and contemporary Ocean Grove.

Are You Being Served?

When you are researching Ocean Grove history and talking to people who vacationed there, the town's restaurants, coffee shops, and cafeterias are often at the top of their list of fond memories. In many ways, time has stood still when it comes to dining in Ocean Grove, as no liquor licenses can be granted to Ocean Grove restaurants, one of the few of the blue laws that remain.

The other portion of the blue laws, among other things, regulated the sale of desserts and ice-cream on Sundays. When the Camp Meeting Association had municipal control, it was against regulations to serve desert on Sunday, unless the person was ordering a full meal. Perhaps this explains why the town's most famous ice-cream parlor, Days, also had a restaurant connected to it.

Days also has the honor of being the longest continuously-operated private establishment in Ocean Grove. Through a long chain of owners, its location on Pittman Avenue, which opened in 1876, has operated through all of the various changes that have evolved at its doorway over the past 130 years. Though you no longer need order a meal to enjoy a Sundae on Sunday, there is an excellent restaurant, The Starving Artist, at Days, which reflects the tastes of modern visitors to Ocean Grove.

The restaurant most often remembered was the Homestead, located in the North End Pavilion, directly over the beach. The Homestead offered American Continental cuisine, served to customers in a dining room decorated in simple colonial elegance. While Ocean Grove was a Victorian community, the restaurant followed the decorating trends of the 1940s and 1950s, which explains the colonial theme to its interior.

When the Homestead closed in the 1970s, the valuable ocean-front space did not stay empty for very long. A Perkins Pancake House® occupied the space for most of the 1980s, carrying forth the tradition of dining at the North End Pavilion. People often remember the bright blue color the walls were painted, and watching waitresses scurry around in a flurry of activity, performing a ballet of chaos on Sundays, never dropping one single pancake on the floor.

This postcard shows the exterior of Days circa 1908.

This view of the interior ice-cream garden is also circa 1908, and looks virtually similar to a visitor today, as it did then. Days also had an annex in Asbury Park, for which this card, depicting the Ocean Grove location is mislabeled for.

The exterior of the Homestead Restaurant shown in this chrome postcard was established in 1915, five years after the North End complex it was attached to was completed.

The interior's expansive ocean views were made possible with the large picture windows. The wait for a table with an ocean or beach view was always the longest. *Courtesy of Judy Ryerson.*

Homestead Restaurant

On the Boardwalk   Ocean Grove, N. J.

The less formal coffee shop at the Homestead was opened in the later years in an attempt to expand and revive lost business.

The bright blue walls of the Ardmore Hotel dining room surround neatly set tables with delicate flower arrangements. The verso of the postcard advertises that it is open to the public, an important piece of information, as many hotels reserved their dining rooms for the exclusive use of their guests.

Hogan's Restaurant and Soda Shoppe were popular amongst residents and visitors alike, at both of the establishment's locations—the one shown here on Main Avenue, and an auxiliary location at the South End Pavilion.

Pioneer-themed décor helps set the mood in this interior view of the Quaker Inn's coffee shop, located on Main Avenue.

The Cozy Cottage, located on Pilgrim Pathway, across from Thornley Chapel, was owned for a number of years by Joseph and Mary Keating, whose son, Ken, now president of the Auditorium Ushers Association, loves hearing the fond memories people have of dining at his parents' restaurant.

The interior of the Cozy Cottage is shown in this chrome era postcard. The Keating family added the catchy slogan to all of their advertisements, "When you think of eating, think of Keating."

Ocean Grove was also known for having an incredible selection of cafeterias; these unique establishments offered a variety of food at reasonable prices. The cafeteria had all but disappeared from American life and Ocean Grove, with the exception of the Sampler Inn, which remained open until a series of unfortunate events lead to its demise a few years ago.

When talking to anyone old enough to have experienced the cafeteria lifestyle in Ocean Grove, they begin to argue amongst themselves as to which cafeteria—or cafeteria item—was better. Some argue ardently for the corn bread that was served at the North End, and some, including this author, fight for the roast round of beef from the Sampler Inn. An entirely separate group will then chime in, arguing the merits of the Grand Atlantic's cafeteria.

FAMOUS FOR GOOD FOOD AT POPULAR PRICES.

Ocean Grove's cafeterias were so popular with visitors that often the line from the Sampler and the Grand Atlantic, located a distance away from each other, would become intertwined as thousands poured out from services in the Auditorium.

WESLAKE CAFETERIA — OCEAN GROVE, N. J.   3A-H552

When it first opened, the North End Cafeteria was known as the Weslake Cafeteria, as shown in this rare deckled edge linen era postcard. *Courtesy of Judy Ryerson.*

MAIN-CENTRAL CAFETERIA and PATIO DINING ROOM

ASBURY PARK

New Branch of
OCEAN GROVE
At 109
Second Avenue

One-Half Block
from Boardwalk

Telephone
Asbury Park 8998

Ocean Grove
Address:
Main and Central
Avenues

Telephone, Asbury Park 8998

Business was so good for the Main-Central Hotel and Cafeteria in the 1920s, that it was forced to expand. Likely faced with a lack of suitable space in Ocean Grove, they chose to add an additional location on Second Avenue in neighboring Asbury Park.

Main-Central Hotels

CAFETERIA SERVICE

109 SECOND AVENUE
ASBURY PARK, N. J.

CORNER MAIN and CENTRAL
AVENUES
OCEAN GROVE, N. J.

EUROPEAN PLAN

Chapter Four
People And Places

By now you've fully enveloped yourself in the history of Ocean Grove, so you should be ready for a quick quiz.

How many streets are in Ocean Grove?

Yes, this is a trick question. The answer is quite surprising; there are only three streets in Ocean Grove: Olin Street, Wall Street and South Main Street. Of the three, only two are actual roads. Wall Street is the name given to the alleyway between the post office building and the building which houses the newspaper store and Ocean Grove Hardware.

All the joking aside, Ocean Grove has a unique collection of people and buildings which make it a special place. Very few locations can rival Ocean Grove for Victorian architecture, and Main Avenue retains a small town charm that attracts visitors to Ocean Grove year round.

Insert a few SUVs and the OGCMA tennis courts and shuffleboard courts into the photo, and this view of the eastern end of Broadway could easily be from today, rather than circa 1911. This is a true testament to historical preservation in Ocean Grove.

The gentleman and child standing on the corner in this white-border image, dated 1930, may have likely stepped off the bus, making the turn from Ocean Avenue onto Broadway. Perhaps they are planning to enjoy some of the concessions present during this time period at the South End Pavilion. *Courtesy of Judy Ryerson.*

The ornate and manicured flower gardens depicted in this linen era view were a trademark of public spaces and parks throughout Ocean Grove. *Courtesy of Judy Ryerson.*

These grand homes alongside Wesley Lake provide a sound impression of the variety of architecture in the Victorian order that is showcased in Ocean Grove. This card has an additional advertisement for the Religious Store, which was located at 518 Cookman Avenue, Asbury Park.

The southern side of Ocean Pathway, showing many of the hotels lost to fire in the 1970s. *Courtesy of Judy Ryerson.*

Greetings from Ocean Grove, N. J.

Main Avenue on a Sunday, with no cars permitted, per the Ocean Grove tradition. The stores on the south side of Main Avenue are also closed, as per the traditions and regulations of Ocean Grove during this period of time.

This chrome era view of Broadway is visually enticing to anyone who appreciates Victorian architecture or classic cars. *Courtesy of Judy Ryerson.*

The Neptune Township High School was located for a number of years at the Main Avenue gates to Ocean Grove. The building, which was completed in 1898, was vacant for a number of years until local residents purchased it from the township, and restored it into a performing arts center.

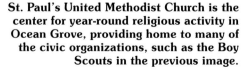

A linen era view of Main and Ocean Avenues; with no cars present in the image, we know this was taken on a Sunday.

St. Paul's United Methodist Church is the center for year-round religious activity in Ocean Grove, providing home to many of the civic organizations, such as the Boy Scouts in the previous image.

69

In this chrome era view, the Belt Line bus is visible, which for a number of years shuttled visitors and residents within Ocean Grove. The North End Hotel was a favorite stop for its passengers. *Courtesy of Judy Ryerson.*

The design of Ocean Grove was very deliberate from the beginning. The trustees laid out the streets in a defined grid pattern, and ensured ocean breezes and ocean views for the first two blocks of each east/west running street. The homes are built with increasing setbacks as you approach Ocean Avenue, and the ends of the blocks flare outwards, creating a funnel effect for the ocean air.

Some of Ocean Grove's streets have names that have obvious connection to their location or purpose, i.e., Ocean Avenue, Broadway, Ocean Pathway, or Main Avenue. The aforementioned Wall Street is named for the literal walls which compose the alleyway. The balance of the streets in Ocean Grove are named either for important figures in the Camp Meeting Association's early history, such as Webb or Lawrence Avenues, or for biblical places, such as Mount Tabor and Mount Zion Ways.

This sepia-toned postcard shows the northern stretch of Ocean Pathway, including the Manchester Hotel.

The western end of Broadway and its residential architecture are not often depicted in postcard scenes. *Courtesy of Judy Ryerson.*

The wide expanse of Ocean Pathway, and the ornate Victorian architecture on either side, has led many people and publications to refer to it as one of the most visually pleasing street scenes in America.

79 — Pittman Avenue — Ocean Grove, N. J.

128:—Abbott Ave., Ocean Grove, N. J.

The lack of vehicles or horses in this real photo postcard leads the viewer to believe it was taken on a Sunday.

Given the quizzical pose taken by the woman in the foreground of this 1930s white border era card, one must assume she has forgotten where she parked. *Courtesy of Judy Ryerson.*

CENTRAL AVENUE, OCEAN GROVE, N. J.

The young woman in this card, showing Central Avenue, seems to have noticed the photographer's presence and is attempting to strike a model-like pose in this white border era card. *Courtesy of Judy Ryerson.*

These streets wind around a collection of Victorian architecture so diverse that only Cape May, New Jersey, can rival. Gothic, Eastlake, and Stick style, are all represented in Ocean Grove. The Luna-Park style of seashore buildings can be seen in the North End Pavilion, a structure that looks just as much at home in Ocean Grove as it would if you picked it up and placed it in an early twentieth century Coney Island postcard.

It is a testament to historical preservation in Ocean Grove that many of the structures viewed in the present look remarkably like the images in historic photographs and postcards. In many views, only the clothing and cars have changed.

This has led to a number of movies being filmed in Ocean Grove. *Stardust Memories*, directed by and staring Woody Allen, is perhaps the most well known. The film used the Great Auditorium as the film's focal point, in addition to filming several scenes in and around Ocean Grove and Asbury Park.

In recognition for being able to film the Auditorium and other parts of Ocean Grove, Woody Allen donated a new memorial cross for the Auditorium. The previous cross was in disrepair, and Allen had it removed as the front of the Auditorium was used as the façade of a Victorian Hotel.

Shopping The Grove

Main Avenue, shown in this chrome era view, is the commercial heart of Ocean Grove, with seventy-five percent of all retail, service, and professional space located along its wide pathway.

Residents and visitors to the area in the early through middle twentieth centuries took care of their banking needs with the Asbury Park and Ocean Grove Bank, with their Asbury Park office shown in this rare postcard. *Courtesy of Judy Ryerson.*

ASBURY PARK AND OCEAN GROVE BANK

ORGANIZED 1889   RESOURCES $3,000,000

The interior of the bank's headquarters, located across from the Ocean Grove and Asbury Park train station. *Courtesy of Judy Ryerson.*

The interior of the Shellcraft shop is shown in this rare postcard, showing the dazzling assortment of sea shells available to its customers. *Courtesy of Judy Ryerson.*

The most important historical fact to consider when looking at the history of commerce in Ocean Grove was the relationship with the Sunday Blue Laws. Per the tradition of the Camp Meeting Association, all stores were closed on Sundays. After the repeal of the blue laws, the stores were allowed to be open on Sundays, but some chose to continue the tradition and remain closed on Sundays.

Starting with the former Ocean Grove Camp Meeting Office building, and continuing east to the restored Nagels building, this card shows the northern side of the commercial corridor of Ocean Grove. *Courtesy of Judy Ryerson.*

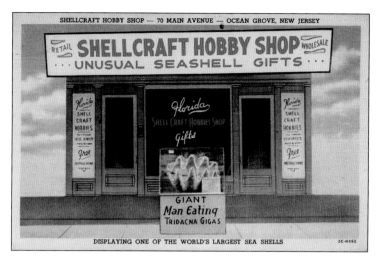

The Shellcraft Hobby Shop, 70 Main Avenue, was well known for this giant clam formerly displayed outside, and then inside, until the business closed a few years ago. *Courtesy of Judy Ryerson.*

Monuments and Memorials

Due in part to the religious background of Ocean Grove, memorials and monuments are plentiful throughout the community, and are some of the most recognizable features of the area. The first monuments a person sees when entering Ocean Grove, depends on whether they have chosen the Main Avenue entrance or Broadway. When entering through Main Avenue, the person passes through a large set of brick gates, which were historically used for setting up the chain on Sundays. The large pillars each have bronze plaques on them, reading, "And Into His Courts With Praise."

Memorial Day ceremonies, like this one from 1956, are a tradition in Ocean Grove. *Courtesy of Milton Edelman.*

Adjacent to this site is the sign that welcomes visitors to Ocean Grove, which initially proclaimed, "God's Square Mile," and was later changed to, "A National Historic Site." The sign's verso calls out to people departing Ocean Grove, the hopeful message of "God Be With You 'Til We Meet Again."

When entering Ocean Grove via Broadway, visitors are greeted by two large granite monuments, each dedicated to war veterans of the first two World Wars and Korea, respectively.

The statue of Dr. Stokes stands guard as a memorial to his service to Ocean Grove in its earliest times.

The memorial urn in Founders Park marks the spot where the first prayer meeting was held in Reverend Thornley's tent in 1869.

The Angel of Victory, shown in this white border era card, was erected as a monument to the struggle overcome during the American Revolution. Damaged beyond repair in a storm in the early 1930s, it is the goal of the Ocean Grove Historical Society to construct a new Angel statue to be placed again at the foot of Main Avenue. *Courtesy of Judy Ryerson.*

PARK SCENE AT MAIN AVE., OCEAN GROVE, N. J.

The fountain in this real photo card, postmarked in 1943, was present when the park was known as Woodlawn Park, prior to the current incarnation of Fireman's Park. *Courtesy of Judy Ryerson.*

Broadway Park, Ocean Grove, N. J.

207N

PHOTO BY AGREEN

87299

The Broadway monuments to both World War I and II soldiers who came from Ocean Grove are depicted in this linen era postcard.

77

This compendium of monuments has firm roots back to Ocean Grove's founders. Stokes and his immediate predecessors stressed the importance of providing things that would beautify and improve the community, while providing the opportunity to reflect upon departed loved ones and God's messages. Since many of the trees which originally filled the site upon which Ocean Grove was developed were removed, the replacement of these trees through planting memorial trees was of utmost importance.

Service To Seniors,
The United Methodist Homes and Ocean Grove.

Service to the senior citizens in Ocean Grove dates back well over 100 years, even prior to the establishment of the United Methodist Homes, who now oversee the operation of the two senior care facilities in Ocean Grove.

Originally known as The Bancroft Taylor Rest Home, it became known as **Clara Swain Manor** when operations were taken over by the United Methodist Homes.

An aerial view of Francis Asbury Manor, slated to be replaced with a modern Victorian structure.

SUNSET REST-BANCROFT-TAYLOR REST HOME, OCEAN GROVE, N. J.

This private home was maintained as part of the Bancroft Taylor facility, and was used for resident's out of town guests in the later years of the home.
Courtesy of Judy Ryerson.

"PALMER HALL," BANCROFT REST HOME, OCEAN GROVE, N. J.

This rare interior view shows the lavish Victorian furniture which residents of this rest home enjoyed.

The newest facility of the United Methodist Homes in Ocean Grove is Manor By The Sea, located at the corner of South Main Street and Stockton Avenue. It was opened in 1995, to replace the aging Clara Swain Manor. Designed to fit in seamlessly with the Victorian architecture of Ocean Grove, it is so attractive on the exterior that during the summer months, people often stop in to inquire about rooms, thinking that it is a hotel! The security staff at the front desk always politely turn them towards the center of town, where they can find an actual hotel or bed and breakfast to stay in.

Parades

Patriotic celebrations have been an integral part of Ocean Grove's summer experience since the town's inception in 1869. Early Camp Meeting reports are filled with references to the combination of religion and patriotism, likely owing a great deal of that towards the religious freedom allowed in America.

Early town-wide celebrations also often included the children's choir of the Great Auditorium, under the direction of Tali Esen Morgan, who had unique ways of dealing with unruly children. He organized the boys' portion of the choir into the Rough Riders Brigade, which was used as a means of controlling their behavior. Organized in a military fashion, they received regular rations of milk and cookies upon the completion of their drills with good behavior.

Morgan was also an early pageant director for Asbury Park's Baby Parade, which often involved use of Ocean Grove during the early part of the twentieth century. When the Asbury Park Casino was destroyed by fire in the 1920s, the town held the crowning of the parade's queen in the Great Auditorium.

In more recent years, parades have become a great source of community pride and spirit, and a large crowd-drawing device. These parades all trace their origin back to the town's first large parade in 1969, which celebrated Ocean Grove's centennial. It was the first major parade to have committees discussing the celebration and festivities for a year or more in advance.

The Centennial Parade featured numerous floats and marching units filled with local residents dressed in Victorian-period clothing. The usual array of marching bands and fire trucks also joined in the festivities of the day.

In recent years the traditional parade route through town has parade traffic moving in the opposite direction than shown in this 1969 Centennial photograph.

Main Avenue, Ocean Grove, N. J.   PHOTO BY McMANUS.

Parades that were associated with children's events in the Auditorium were often popular during the early twentieth century.

A marching band and its colorful uniforms are depicted in this photograph of the 1969 Centennial Parade.

Many of the groups associated with Ocean Grove, such as the Board of Trustees, shown in this image from 1969, often march in the town's Fourth of July parade.

The colorful period costumes were an added attraction to the 1969 parade.

Firetruck from the parade.

The 1969 parade ushered in a generation's worth of parades celebrating both Independence Day, and many Ocean Grove institutions that would, soon, also be hitting the hundred-year mark. These included: The E. H. Stokes Fire Department Centennial, 1986; The Thornley Chapel Centennial, 1988; and The Auditorium Centennial, which also served to honor the 125th Anniversary of Ocean Grove, 1994.

The driving force behind these parades over the years has been the Ocean Grove Camp Meeting Association's Parade Committee, led for a number of years by Herb Noack, who has assembled some of the largest parades that Ocean Grove has ever seen.

Antique bicycles are a popular attraction in any parade, such as these from the 1969 parade. *Courtesy of Rip Mohl.*

Hotels often are called upon to sponsor marching bands and other units in the Ocean Grove parade. *Courtesy of Rip Mohl.*

The Ocean Grove Hotel Association's banner is shown in this photograph. *Courtesy of Rip Mohl.*

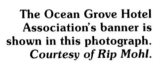

In recent years, one of most popular floats was that of the group, Save Tillie, who had been working to preserve the landmark Palace Amusements in neighboring Asbury Park.

Chapter Five
Ocean and Lakes

The presence of the Atlantic Ocean was a large factor in the success of Ocean Grove. The ability to cool off in the fresh salt water made Ocean Grove more attractive to a late nineteenth century visitor than say, a landlocked Camp Meeting Ground. While bathing suits have changed substantially over the last 135 years, the Ocean's lure hasn't, and in contemporary Ocean Grove, it is just as important to both the religious and secular sides of the town.

This unique panel view postcard shows Ross' Pavilion and its other ancillary structures, which included a bookstore and a restaurant.

Ocean Grove's boardwalk was an important first step in the development of the community, and was partly a reflection upon the fashion of the era. The large, voluminous, skirts worn by Victorian women were not conducive for wearing in the sand. As a result of this problem, which also existed in other seashore resorts coming to life in this time period, such as Atlantic City and Asbury Park, wooden walkways were laid down upon the sand dunes. This allowed the ladies to stroll along the shore, taking in fresh salt water air, and watching the sights and sounds of the rolling surf.

This card poses a puzzling question, what happened to the boardwalk railing? In various images, all from the early twentieth century, sometimes it's there, sometimes it isn't. The only plausible explanation is that in between repairs from storms or other damage, it was removed to facilitate the repair work. *Courtesy of Judy Ryerson.*

One of the earliest uses of the Ocean Grove beach was not recreational bathing, but as a place for a congregation to gather to listen to a sermon being preached from the boardwalk. Hopefully, services were held at low tide, lest anyone receive an unexpected surfside baptism.

Strolling along the boardwalk, as shown in this postcard from 1905, has been a popular pastime since the inception of the boardwalk generations ago. *Courtesy of Judy Ryerson.*

The people in charge of public facilities in all communities quickly saw the universal appeal of the boardwalk, and began making them permanent structures. Ocean Grove's boardwalk was made a permanent structure in the late nineteenth century, and has remained a popular feature ever since.

The lifeguard chair is empty in this hand-colored litho-chrome postcard, leading the viewer to believe that the diligent life guards are in the midst of a daring rescue. *Courtesy of Judy Ryerson.*

This sign was posted along the boardwalk to remind visitors of the regulations for bathing on Sunday. This example, from the author's collection, was produced prior to the regulations being relaxed to allow the beach to be open after 12:00 pm on Sunday; this is to allow undisturbed Sunday worship in the Auditorium.

Why the young gentleman is standing up on top of that pole is better left as a distant mystery of wonder. Looking through the image, you also catch a glimpse of the dapper red- and white-striped uniforms worn by early twentieth century Ocean Grove life guards. *Courtesy of Judy Ryerson.*

The fishing pier was added to the end of Embury Avenue in 1891. *Courtesy of Judy Ryerson.*

These young boys and men all seem to be enjoying finding out what the catch of the day will be in this circa 1925 white border era postcard. *Courtesy of Judy Ryerson.*

86

Kiddies on the Beach at Ocean Grove, N. J.

These young twin boys and girls are enjoying what appears to be a Mickey Mouse sand bucket. *Courtesy of Judy Ryerson.*

Hello from Ocean Grove, N. J.

There has always been great rivalry and separation between which beaches Ocean Grove residents and visitors prefer. This group of bathers, under colorful umbrellas, obviously preferred the South End bathing beach. *Courtesy of Judy Ryerson.*

BEACH SCENE AT NORTH END, OCEAN GROVE, N. J.

The North End bathing beach is depicted in this sepia-toned postcard.

Ocean Grove, N. J.

The flagpole at the foot of Embury Avenue also served double duty as the ventilation for the town's sanitary sewer system.

Surfing has been a popular recreational activity in Ocean Grove since it was first allowed in the 1970s. *Courtesy of Judy Ryerson.*

Ocean Grove, N. J.

The North and South Ends of Ocean Grove.

The presence of lakes forming the northern and southern boarders of Ocean Grove offered natural isolation, integral to Ocean Grove's success as a place of relaxation. Originally known as Long Pond (now Wesley Lake), and Duck Pond (now Fletcher Lake), they have been a source for amusement and recreation since the town's inception in 1869.

The boarders of Wesley Lake were historically home to the only commercial amusements allowed along the Ocean Grove waterfront. The North End Hotel's ancillary facilities held a merry-go-round, a movie theater, skeeball, a shooting gallery, and a bowling alley.

A view of the South End beach, looking towards Bradley Beach. *Courtesy of Judy Ryerson.*

Long boards, such as the one shown in this postcard, were preferred by surfers who were more adept and used to the sport. *Courtesy of Judy Ryerson.*

The structure at the beginning of the pier was used by the fishing club's members to sell fish they caught off the end of the pier. *Courtesy of Judy Ryerson.*

LANDING OF FISHING BOAT, LOOKING TOWARD OCEAN GROVE, N. J.

Prior to the development of major inlets around the area, small fishing boats like this one, often brought their catch right up onto the beach. *Courtesy of Judy Ryerson.*

A group of bathing beauties seems to have caught the eye of a gentleman in this postcard. *Courtesy of Judy Ryerson.*

On the Beach, Ocean Grove, N. J.

9091

A family enjoys the beach in this white border postcard. *Courtesy of Judy Ryerson.*

A crowded beach has been a common sight in Ocean Grove since the town first assigned bathing rights to a concessionaire in 1876. *Courtesy of Judy Ryerson.*

Scene on the Beach from South End Pavilion, Ocean Grove, N. J.

Add to this mixture a number of concession stands, both at boardwalk level and within the North End Pavilion, and you have a central core of memories for three generations of residents and visitors. The popularity of the amusements at the North End was certainly helped by neighboring Asbury Park, with the Casino linking both boardwalks, and decadent places of amusement, such as Palace Amusements, luring Ocean Grover's over.

A view of early North End concessions, including the Morris Kodak studio, the creators of many now valuable and rare real photo postcards dating from the early twentieth century. *Courtesy of Judy Ryerson.*

This early view of the pavilion and hotel shows both the Asbury Park Casino, a seamless part of the North End, and the concession stands famous for their engraved leather and glass souvenirs. *Courtesy of Judy Ryerson.*

The South End had a pavilion, originally known as Lillagore's, which contained bath houses and concessions. The bath houses here, and at the North End, were especially important, because for a number of years the Association's regulations prohibited the wearing of bathing attire in public, outside of the confines of the ocean and beach. The South End Pavilion was expanded using lumber from the Auditorium of 1880, which was dismantled to make way for the Great Auditorium of 1894.

Arthur Livingston, Publisher, New York. 341

LILLAGORE'S PAVILION, OCEAN GROVE, N.J.

A similar view of Lillagore's Pavilion; the sender of this divided back era card talks about watching the bathers and people strolling—postmarked in 1911. *Courtesy of Judy Ryerson.*

Lillagore Pavilion, Ocean Grove, N, J.

Lillagore's Pavilion, located at the southern end of Ocean Grove's boardwalk, was expanded to the size shown in this Arthur Livingston postcard using lumber salvaged from the Auditorium of 1880.

93

Ocean Grove, N.J.

Fletcher Lake is an integral part of life at the south end of Ocean Grove. Here a little boy docks his rowboat on the Bradley Beach side of the lake, and the South End Pavilion is visible in the distance.

SOUTH END BEACH and Boardwalk, Ocean Grove, N. J.

176

The boardwalk continued out around the pavilion structure, allowing for leisurely viewing of the ocean and beach scenes.

Ocean Avenue and South End Pavilion, Ocean Grove, N. J.   128

The person who sent this linen era card remarks that the pavilion, which still contained elements of Lillagore's late-nineteenth century structure, was washed away in the Great Atlantic Hurricane of 1944.

Fletcher Lake, Ocean Grove, N.J.

126:—Boating on Fletcher Lake, showing Ocean Grove, N.J.

The footbridge over Fletcher Lake shown in this picture was located towards the eastern end of the lake, and was likely destroyed in a storm and never replaced. Also visible in this card, postmarked 1910, is the famous Kent family mansion in Bradley Beach. *Courtesy of Judy Ryerson.*

The footbridge, still existing today, is shown in this white border era view, postmarked in 1931. Rebuilt several times over the years, most recently in 1992, the tents which Francis Asbury Manor replaced are shown in this unique image. *Courtesy of Judy Ryerson.*

Postmarked in 1931, this white border era card shows renovations applied to the South End Pavilion, likely to allow it to blend better with the competing North End Pavilion. *Courtesy of Judy Ryerson.*

BEACH, SOUTH END, OCEAN GROVE, N. J.

Ocean Grove. N. J.

Shuffle board has been a popular recreation at the South End of Ocean Grove for years. These courts are also augmented by tennis courts and a playground. *Courtesy of Judy Ryerson.*

North End Amusements

The first swimming pool located at the North End was operated as part of Ross' bathing establishment, and is shown in this litho chrome postcard, before the pool was relocated, to facilitate the expansion of the North End Hotel. *Courtesy of Judy Ryerson.*

A rare real photo postcard of the North End prior to the construction of the North End Hotel in 1910. Ross' Pavilion and the Bethesda tents are visible, as well as a small structure with a swooping roofline, used to sell tickets to Auditorium events. This structure still survives, located on Heck Avenue; it now serves as a diminutive summer cottage. *Courtesy of Judy Ryerson.*

A linen era view of the North End swimming pool that was in operation until structural problems led to its abandonment in the 1980s. Many Ocean Grove residents and visitors who came in the 1950s and 1960s remember the swimming lessons given by Dr. Anna Nichols, a longtime Ocean Grove summer resident. *Courtesy of Judy Ryerson.*

While amusements and commercial structures were not allowed along the main stretch of boardwalk, commerce was greatly encouraged in both the North and South Ends of the boardwalk. The North End Hotel complex was the primary location for amusements in Ocean Grove, and was also right next to Asbury Park, famous for its boardwalk amusements. The Ocean Grove Sunday Blue Laws meant that all of the North End's attractions were closed on Sundays, so it is highly likely that on Sundays, and other times too, Ocean Grove's youth snuck through the Casino to experience the fun on the other side of the lake.

The North End Hotel's amusements included; The Strand Theater, The Merry-Go-Round, The Skee-Ball Alley, and The Shooting Gallery. These were all located on the northern facade of the building, overlooking Wesley Lake. Several famous concessions were also poised in this location, ready to make the tourists, and locals for that matter, part with their hard-earned cash. Amongst this long list of businesses were Khors Frozen Custard, and the portraiture studio owned and operated by Zad, as well as the Macaroon Shop.

Wesley Lake served as a shared arena of amusement, with such famous attractions as the Swan Boat, motor boats, and U-Pedal Boats, all appearing at different times during the height of both Asbury Park and Ocean Grove's popularity.

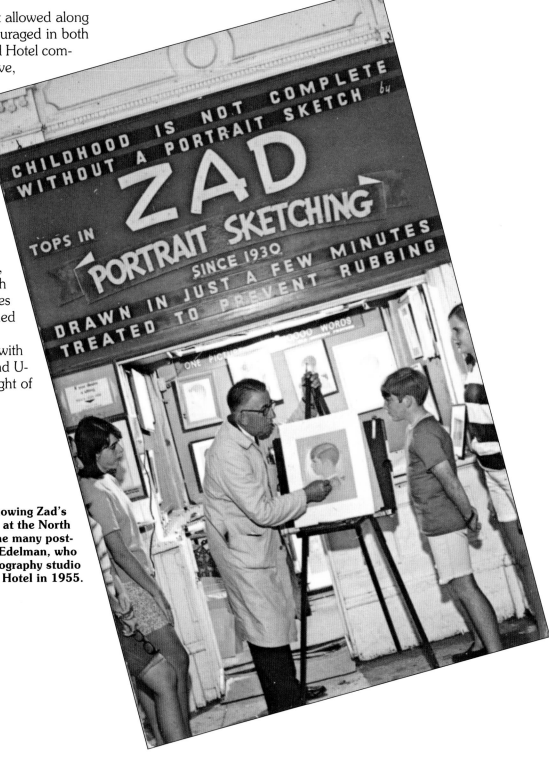

The concession stand showing Zad's portraiture studio, located at the North End Hotel. This is one of the many postcards produced by Milton Edelman, who opened his commercial photography studio in Asbury Park's Monterey Hotel in 1955.

The Strand Theater was located in the eastern most corner of the North End Hotel. Built in the first phase of construction, it was initially known as the Scenario, and it too followed in the Sunday-closing tradition. When the theater was remodeled, a number of the original wooden theater seats were transferred to the balcony of the Auditorium, where they remain today. Like many of the movie palaces in neighboring Asbury Park, the interior of the Strand Theater is not well documented in photography. This is likely due to difficulties in flash photography in the early part of the twentieth century.

The Ocean Grove Merry-Go-Round was installed in 1911, as one of the final steps in the construction of the massive North End Hotel Complex. It was hand carved from wood by The Dentzel Carousel Co.; a company based in Philadelphia Pennsylvania, and featured a full menagerie of animals besides the traditional horses. This carousel was unique because the platform on which the animals rode was on two levels, with the jumping horses located a single step higher than the stationary animals on the outside of the ride.

Bridge over Wesley Lake, Asbury Park, N. J.

The iron footbridge over Wesley Lake is shown in this postcard, which was likely closed since the newspaper stand is not open—probably taken on a Sunday.

WESLEY LAKE. OCEAN GROVE AND ASBURY PARK, N. J.

This rare sepia-toned image features a painter working on the advertisements for various Camp Meeting programs on the retaining wall along Wesley Lake. *Courtesy of Judy Ryerson.*

The Emory Street Bridge, Ocean Grove, N. J.

A view of the iron footbridge over Wesley Lake, obviously not taken on a Sunday, as the newspaper stand is in full operation. *Courtesy of Judy Ryerson.*

NORTH END PAVILION, OCEAN GROVE.

The North End Pavilion was the first structure to open at the North End of Ocean Grove as part of the North End Hotel complex.

Ocean Grove, N. J.

Under this stretch of boardwalk was an entrance to a subterranean tunnel which led to the changing rooms and bath houses located within the North End Complex.

The northern façade of the hotel, showing the Strand Theater and other famous concessions.

BOARDWALK AT NORTH END PAVILION, OCEAN GROVE, N. J.
OCEAN GROVE

The Excursionists Pavilion
was offered for people
who wished a place to eat
a picnic lunch brought
with them from home.

NORTH END HOTEL   OCEAN GROVE, N. J.

An early view of the hotel,
with the pony rides that
were once located on the
border between the Ocean
Grove and Asbury Park
boardwalks.

WESLEY LAKE AT NORTH END HOTEL, OCEAN GROVE, N. J.

A view of the many popular concessions along the northern side of the North End Complex.

The swan boat and motor boats were popular shared attractions in Wesley Lake.

Swan and Motor Boat Rides on Wesley Lake. Asbury Park and Ocean Grove, N. J.

ATLANTIC CITY, N.J.
WILLOW GROVE, PA.
WOODSIDE PARK, PHILA., PA.
AND ALL OTHER PARKS.

An advertising postcard produced by the Dentzel Carousel Company, who created the North End Merry-Go-Round.
The model depicted in this postcard is similar to the one formerly located at the North End, and shows many of the
unique animals that people who rode it fondly remember.

Heck St. Bridge, Wesley Lake, Asbury Park and Ocean Grove, N. J.

We are having a nice time. Lillian

A view from the lake of the iron footbridge with the Sheldon House in the background. *Courtesy of Judy Ryerson.*

HECK STREET BRIDGE OVER WESLEY LAKE. OCEAN GROVE, N. J.   142

These concrete bridges replaced the older iron foot bridges in 1929.

Beautiful Scene on Wesley Lake, Ocean Grove, N. J.

A view of the western end of the lake, with the Weeping Willow trees that provide shade alongside the lake.

Wesley Lake, Asbury Park, N. J.

A view of the lake prior to the construction of the concrete retaining wall that coincided with the construction of the North End Hotel.

7:—Wesley Lake, Ocean Grove, N. J.

This white border view shows the grand Victorian homes alongside the western portion of Wesley Lake.

105

The change in elevation is evident along the lake's banks in this real photo postcard.

Having a glorious time. Wish for you often. B.P.

A GLIMPSE OF WESLEY LAKE, OCEAN GROVE, N. J.

Arthur Livingston, Publisher, New York

4:—Wesley Lake showing Asbury Park and Ocean Grove, N. J.

While most commercial amusements were located on the Asbury Park side of Wesley Lake, this postcard shows that in addition to the Merry-Go-Round, a bumper-car ride also existed at the North End Complex for a period of time. *Courtesy of Judy Ryerson.*

WESLEY LAKE BETWEEN ASBURY PARK AND OCEAN GROVE, N. J.

The space occupied by the pony track attraction in this card was soon replaced with the Art Deco structure that served as the power plant for Asbury Park's boardwalk.

106

An unusual view of the railing installed along the western most banks of Wesley Lake,
designed to match the footbridges of the same time period. *Courtesy of Judy Ryerson.*

THE
HECK STREET
BRIDGE
WESLEY ESPLANADE -
TO NORTH END
OCEAN GROVE, N.J.

A photograph showing the Heck Street Bridge has been inset into this card.

Chapter Six
Fire and Fury

With one of the nation's largest repositories of Victorian architecture, Ocean Grove residents are fortunate to have one of the finest volunteer fire and first aide departments at their service. The communities' need for fire protection requires Ocean Grove to have one of the largest collections of fire fighting apparatus per-capita, as compared to other neighboring communities.

This Chevrolet Utility Truck served the Ocean Grove Fire Police, a group that provides extra manpower by diverting traffic and pedestrians during fires and other emergencies.

In 1928, this seventy-five foot American La France truck began serving the Eagle Hook and Ladder Company. The articulated truck body allowed it to navigate the narrow streets of Ocean Grove with ease. *Courtesy of Judy Ryerson.*

This International Tasco engine served the Washington Fire Co. No. 1, which shares space with the Stokes' Firehouse on Central and Olin Avenues. *Courtesy of Judy Ryerson.*

This circa 1950s truck served the E. H. Stokes Fire Co., No. 3. Of note, on this engine is the early styled Municipal "MG" Government license plate. *Courtesy of Judy Ryerson.*

The Ocean Grove First Aide Squad was established in 1935; prior to that time, first-aide equipment was carried on the Stokes' Company engines. This is one of the department's ambulances from the 1950s—a Cadillac. *Courtesy of Judy Ryerson.*

This 1951 Packard Ambulance served Ocean Grove's First Aide Squad. *Courtesy of Judy Ryerson.*

This 1912 American LaFrance ladder truck was one of the first vehicles to serve the Eagle Hook and Ladder Company. *Courtesy of Judy Ryerson.*

The Fountain House Hotel fire was one of the largest fires the Ocean Grove Fire Department's had to face in its early history. The hotel is shown on fire in this rare image, from 1918, with the silhouettes of Ocean Grove's bravest battling the great conflagration. *Courtesy of Judy Ryerson.*

A number of early fires in Ocean Grove's history were documented with postcards. While it is hard to believe that the average tourist would have wanted to remember a tragedy such as a fire, postcards were often used as a means of communicating news between residents and their faraway relatives.

The smoldering ruins of the fire are shown in this post-card, with The Youth Temple now visible where porches were once visible.

This great fire, which affected the North End Hotel March 7, 1938, spared the carousel and other amusements from any serious damage. These disaster postcards were, at their time, a very efficient means of communicating images relating to such events. This card was produced very quickly, as it is postmarked on March 10, 1938, just three days after the fire occurred.

The Polonaise Hotel before the fire which destroyed the hotel.

The Polonaise Hotel, Main Avenue, was destroyed by fire in the early 1990s. The fire also damaged the adjacent Imperial House Hotel.

Not all events that the Ocean Grove Fire Departments respond to are emergencies involving fire. The departments responded to the collapse of the Queen Hotel in November 1995. The structure had been abandoned for a number of years, and was in the process of being renovated, when a strong fall storm caused the weakened structure to collapse.

While the Polonaise was demolished immediately, the Imperial's demolition took a while longer, as initially, it was thought the structure could be saved.

HOTEL   Imperial

Being primarily a summer resort, postcards depicting snow fall are comparatively rare. This postcard captures a fresh snowfall upon the grounds of the Bancroft Taylor Rest Home. *Courtesy of Judy Ryerson.*

This angry ocean was the result of the storm which caused the Blizzard of 1996, which placed Ocean Grove under a record snowfall.

The beauty and benefits of the Atlantic Ocean have been a drawing point of the town since the first prayer service in 1869. It has also been a source of destruction at times, when Mother Nature's fury rages forth from the depths of the sea. When speaking of the town's history, people often recall the spectacular storms of years gone by, including the 1944 hurricane, Hurricane Gloria, and the December 1992 North Eastern storm. Delving further back into the history of Ocean Grove, into The Camp Meeting reports from the late 1890s, mention is made of several storms that devastated the town's boardwalk during this early time period.

Storms present a constant threat to all structures built alongside the ocean. Here a lone individual surveys the damage to the North End Pavilion and pier after a winter storm in 1914. *Courtesy of Judy Ryerson.*

This washout was caused by a late fall storm in November 1953. *Courtesy of Judy Ryerson.*

This photograph depicts a shop owner's response to this storm; the lucky ones that still *had* shops, offered things like the flood-damaged goods sale here at the Ocean Grove Linen Shop.

This postcard shows the large amounts of debris scattered through the arcade walk between the North End Hotel and Pavilion.

North End Hotel and Boardwalk, Ocean Grove, N. J. Hurricane of Sept. 14, 1944

The Ocean Grove Fishing Pier was completely destroyed during the 1992 December Nor'easter.

One of the boardwalk's trademark benches is shown here during the storm, ripped from the boardwalk and buried in two feet of sand and debris.

Taken a few months after the storm, in March 1993, this photograph shows the destruction of the boardwalk looking south towards the fishing pier.

The boardwalk was completely destroyed in the 1944 Great Atlantic Hurricane, shown here looking north along Ocean Avenue, from about the foot of Main Avenue. *Courtesy of Judy Ryerson.*

The North End Hotel and Pavilion suffered severe damage from the 1944 Hurricane, as shown in this photograph. *Courtesy of Judy Ryerson.*

There's a ship burning off Ocean Pathway.
The Morro-Castle Disaster.

The quiet morning air of Ocean Grove was pierced with the cries of, "There's a ship burning off Ocean Pathway!" It was September 8, 1934, and it was the ill fated Morro Castle that had caught fire. Many of the survivors had already come ashore just south of Ocean Grove in Spring Lake and Manasquan.

It was in the process of being towed towards New York, where the remains of the deceased would be removed from the still-smoldering hulk, prior to the ship being scrapped. Soon after passing Ocean Grove, the Morro Castle, being blown in towards the shore, ran aground on a sand bar, just off Asbury Park's Convention Hall. Several unsuccessful attempts were made to remove the ship in the days immediately following the disaster. It was eventually removed months later, after becoming a macabre tourist attraction for the area. Some historians and scholars actually point to the revenue generated by these tourists as a reason for the Asbury Park area recovering quickly from the Great Depression.

This rare poetry card was produced to commemorate the Moro Castle disaster and features a photograph of the doomed ship.

S. S. Morro Castle

Ship

Disaster

On the Eighth of September, Nineteen Thirty-four
The good ship Morro Castle, all afire went ashore,
On Asbury Park Beach, while a storm was raging high
And all through the city you could hear an alarming cry.
We will always remember this great disaster and strife;
Let us also remember many loved ones lost their life.

---Weston.

Copyrighted 1934 by Charles B. Weston

Chapter Seven

Notable Neighbors

Asbury Park, Bradley Beach, Neptune Township...
    Ocean Grove has also been an integral part of the surrounding community, and is today a part of Neptune Township, following the court decision removing municipal control from the Camp Meeting Association. Neptune Township has been a source of commerce and recreation for Ocean Grove since the very beginning of the Township.

VIEW FROM SKY TOP, SHARK RIVER HILLS, N. J.

FROM SKY TOP CAN BE SEEN ASBURY PARK, OCEAN GROVE, SPRING LAKE AND THE ATLANTIC OCEAN.

This postcard depicts one of the highest points in Neptune Township, the Shark River Hills section. When builders were developing the land during the early part of the twentieth century, they billed it as "The New Asbury Park Suburb." *Courtesy of Judy Ryerson.*

This postcard depicts Storyland's take on the story of *Little Miss Muffet.* **Courtesy of Judy Ryerson.**

Visitors to the Ocean Grove area who preferred a more rustic, camping-like, environment, could have stayed at the Eldridge Tourist Camp, which was located on Rte. 33 and 35 in Neptune Township.

Storyland Village was located on Rte. 66 in Neptune Township, and featured over fifty acres of living storybook village scenes and children's amusement park rides. This structure was King Arthur's Court, which served as the park's main entrance. *Courtesy of Judy Ryerson.*

As travel by automobile became more popular during the twentieth century, people who came to the Ocean Grove area who were also enjoying the start of the RV culture could have parked their vintage streamlined trailers at Eldridge as well.

Ocean Grove has been connected with Asbury Park, beyond simple geography, since James Bradley, Asbury Park's founder, bought the first lot in Ocean Grove in 1870. Seven years later he would establish Asbury Park, a non-sectarian resort, but with regulations so as to not interfere with the religious nature of Ocean Grove.

It is highly likely that many Ocean Grove residents crossed over the Wesley Lake foot bridges on Sundays, to either shop, see a movie, or go for a ride on one of the two wonderful carousels formerly located on the Asbury side of Wesley Lake.

Asbury Park was also the home to many large businesses which were integral to Ocean Grove. The famous department store of Steinbach's provided homeowners and hotel owners with countless amounts of goods and supplies. It was also home to the Road Ad Service Sign Company, whose sign work in Ocean Grove also included the famous Memorial Cross on the exterior of the Great Auditorium.

The Asbury Park attractions alongside Wesley Lake were often synonymously grouped with those in Ocean Grove. *Courtesy of Judy Ryerson.*

The Palace and Mayfair Theater were open on Sundays, when all of Ocean Grove's North End amusements were closed. Likely, more than a few Ocean Grove teens during this time period may have been seen sneaking over the lake to enjoy a movie or a merry-go-round ride on Sunday! *Courtesy of Judy Ryerson.*

MR. ARTHUR PRYOR.
ASBURY PARK'S POPULAR BANDMASTER.
"ON JERSEY SHORE"

"The man you left behind you." Dead.

Arthur Livingston, Publisher, New York, 892

Arthur Pryor got his start in John Phillip Sousa's Marching Band, and grew to unprecedented popularity in the early twentieth century, playing numerous concerts in Ocean Grove and Asbury Park.

WESLEY LAKE, FROM OCEAN GROVE

Bathing was excellent, fine weather. Lovingly, annie

Palace Amusements, which initially included a carousel and Ferris Wheel, was a part of the skyline of Wesley Lake from when it opened in 1888, through its closing in 1988. Despite being listed on the National and New Jersey Registers of Historic Places, the building was demolished in May 2004.

WESLEY LAKE

A view from atop the Palace's Ferris Wheel, showing the gazebo which was located in Founders Park in Ocean Grove.

Asbury Park, N. J.

Prior to their removal in the 1970s, this Mississippi River Steamer-styled boat joined the famous Swan Boat in Wesley Lake.

The original Asbury Park Casino, which was destroyed by fire in the 1920s. While plans and construction were underway for the present Casino, many Asbury Park sponsored events utilized the Great Auditorium in Ocean Grove.

THE CASINO, ASBURY PARK, N.J.

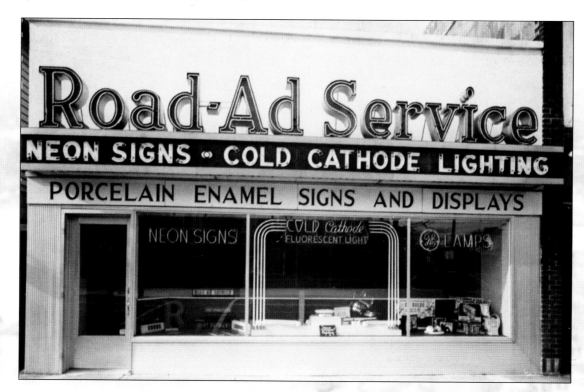

The Road Ad Sign Company was responsible for numerous signs in and around Ocean Grove and Asbury Park. Their most recognizable contribution to the Ocean Grove landscape was that of the Memorial Cross on the front of the Auditorium.

The Casino, a landmark structure which was designed by the New York firm of Warren and Whetmore, opened in 1930, replacing an earlier wooden structure which burned down.

127

Bibliography

Bell, Wayne T., *Images of America: Ocean Grove*. Charleston, South Carolina: Arcadia Publishing, an imprint of Tempus Publishing Inc., 2000.

Bell, Wayne T., and Flynn, Christopher, *Images of America: Ocean Grove In Vintage Postcards*. Charleston, South Carolina: Arcadia Publishing, an imprint of Tempus Publishing Inc., 2004.

Pike, Helen-Chantal, *Greetings From New Jersey, A Postcard Tour of The Garden State*. New Brunswick, New Jersey: Rutgers University Press, 2001.

Savadore, Larry, and Buchholz, Margaret Thomas, *Great Storms of the Jersey Shore*. Harvey Cedars, New Jersey: Down The Shore Publishing, 1993.

Turner, James Lincoln, *Seven Superstorms of the Northeast And Other Blizzards, Hurricanes and Tempests*. Harvey Cedars, New Jersey: Down The Shore Publishing, 2005.

Various, *Four Score and Five—1879-1964 Township of Neptune, New Jersey*, Neptune Township, New Jersey: The Neptune Township Tercentenary Committee, 1964.